The Beginner's Guide to Praise and Worship

The Beginner's Guide to Praise and Worship

GARY KINNAMAN

VINE
BOOKS

SERVANT PUBLICATIONS
ANN ARBOR, MICHIGAN

Vine Books is an imprint of Servant Publications especially designed to serve evangelical Christians.

Servant Mission Statement
We are dedicated to publishing books that spread the gospel of Jesus Christ,
help Christians to live in accordance with that gospel, promote renewal in
the church, and bear witness to Christian unity.

Scripture quotations are taken from the Holy Bible, New International Version.
Copyright 1973, 1978, 1984 by International Bible Society. Used by permission
of Zondervan Publishing House. All rights reserved.

Published by Servant Publications
P.O. Box 8617
Ann Arbor, Michigan 48107
www.servantpub.com

Cover design by Alan Furst, Inc. Minneapolis, Minn.

03 04 05 06 10 9 8 7 6 5 4 3

Printed in the United States of America
ISBN 1-56955-336-X

Library of Congress Cataloging-in-Publication Data

Kinnaman, Gary.
  The beginner's guide to praise and worship / Gary Kinnaman.
     p. cm.
  ISBN 1-56955-336-X (alk. paper)
  1. Worship. I. Title.
  BV10.3 .K56 2003
  248.3--dc21

                                                              2002155465

Contents

1. ONE THING MORE THAN ANYTHING
Why worship is the most important thing in life. / 7

2. BEHOLD YOUR GOD!
Who is the God we worship? / 21

3. HOLY AWE
Holy, Holy, Holy. God in Three Persons,
blessed Trinity. / 35

4. YOU HAD TO BE THERE
How we literally encounter and experience God in worship. / 51

5. TRANSFORMATION
Encountering God's presence in worship heals,
restores, and changes us forever. / 61

6. PERFECT JESUS, TAKE MY HAND
Worship is not something we do for God;
it's what God does in us and through us. / 73

7. WHOLEHEARTED, FULL-BODIED PRAISE
How to praise the Lord, how to worship God. / 87

8. MONDAY WORSHIP
Worship isn't just singing really special songs;
it's everything you do. / 105

9. WARFARE WORSHIP
The necessity and power of worship in spiritual warfare. / 115

10. PRACTICING PRAISE
Getting you into God's presence right where you are. / 127

NOTES / 139

ONE

ONE THING MORE THAN ANYTHING

*One thing I ask of the Lord, this is what I seek: that I may
dwell in the house of the Lord all the days of my life, to gaze
upon the beauty of the Lord and to seek him in his temple.*

PSALM 27:4

The World Series! *We're at the World Series!*" I screamed at
my wife, Marilyn.

I had to scream! The place was rockin'!

We love baseball, we're over fifty, and this was a first for both
of us. After just four years in the league, the Arizona Diamond-
backs were playing the New York Yankees in the unforget-
table fall of 2001. You know, the fall of the World Trade Center
towers. And now our hometown was being swept away in the
great river of American tradition and the flood of tragedy and
emotion.

I had begged my friend David for tickets. Having mercy on
his poor pastor, he took us to the sixth game. The seats were
way out there in left field, behind the bleachers, the last row
before "standing room only." *But we were there!*

More than an hour before the game, the stadium was thump-
ing with sound and electric with energy and emotion. After fifteen runs and a whopping lead in just five innings, everyone had
a reason to go home early. Yet this was the World Series! No one

left the ballpark until long after the last out. We strutted to our car, exhilarated by the win but emotionally drained from nearly four hours of nonstop baseball madness.

Fine Christian leader that I am, I'm ashamed to admit that this event was one of the most extraordinary experiences of my life. In fact, I can't remember anything quite like it ... except ... well ...

The night I was in another stadium a few years ago in Cali, Columbia. Forty thousand people inside, not an empty seat in the house, and a crush of ten thousand people outside, still trying to get in. No, it wasn't a World Cup soccer match. It was a monster prayer and praise service, and these Christian believers came to worship God literally *all night*. Like the World Series, nobody left early, not even the ten thousand in "standing room only" outside the stadium.

Just to be with God.

Years ago, before the fall of communism in Eastern Europe, I preached to a standing-room-only crowd in a midweek service in a huge church in Oradia, Romania. A couple thousand people were standing, not because all the seats were taken, but because they had taken all of the seats right out of the building so more people could crowd into the house of God. There they stood, jammed shoulder to shoulder, men on one side of the room, women on the other, for two hours.

Just to be with God.

One Thing More Than Anything ...

Is there something inside you wanting desperately to know and experience more of God? Are you longing for the indescribable joy of being in the presence of the Lord of the universe? Are you yearning for an encounter with eternity, where time stands still and your life is changed forever? St. Anselm wrote, "Let me seek Thee in longing; let me long for thee in seeking; let me find thee in love, and love thee in finding."

Known as a man after God's own heart, King David declared, "One thing I ask of the Lord, this is what I seek: that I may dwell in the house of the Lord all the days of my life, to gaze upon the beauty of the Lord and to seek him in his temple" (Ps 27:4). Only one thing: *just to be with God.* As the much-quoted Westminster Confession of Faith declares, our "chief end is to glorify God and to enjoy him forever." Listen to King David again:

> *Praise be to you, O Lord, God of our father Israel, from ever-lasting to everlasting. Yours, O Lord, is the greatness and the power and the glory and the majesty and the splendor, for everything in heaven and earth is yours. Yours, O Lord, is the kingdom; you are exalted as head over all. Wealth and honor come from you; you are the ruler of all things. In your hands are strength and power to exalt and give strength to all. Now, our God, we give you thanks, and praise your glorious name. But who am I, and who are my people, that we should be able to give as generously as this? Everything comes from you, and we have given you only what comes from your hand.*
> 1 Chronicles 29:10-14

Maybe right now, in this moment, you're alone in some place where you can read aloud David's extraordinary exclamation of praise. Or maybe you can at least whisper it softly to yourself. Go ahead. This is a book about praise and worship, so let's get right into it! Use this passage *right now* to talk to God. After each sentence, close your eyes for a few moments to reflect on its meaning. Tell God how much you love and adore him. Tell him how much you need him in your life. Welcome his presence. Let the healing of his holy nearness flow into your anxious thoughts and troubled emotions.

So, Who Do We Think We Are?

Do you feel a little unworthy during intense times with God? Even insignificant? Take heart—King David did, too. At the end of his praise song he feels like he is at the end of himself: "But who am I," he concludes in humility, "and who are my people?" (1 Chr 29:14). *So, who do we think we are?* Especially when we consider God. You, O Lord ...

> ... *our Lord, how majestic is your name in all the earth! You have set your glory above the heavens. From the lips of children and infants you have ordained praise because of your enemies, to silence the foe and the avenger. When I consider your heavens, the work of your fingers, the moon and the stars, which you have set in place, what is man that you are mindful of him?*
>
> PSALM 8:1-4

So, just who do we think we are? One of the best-loved Christian writers of the last hundred years, A.W. Tozer, answered the question in his book *Whatever Happened to Worship:* "Yes, worship of the loving God is our whole reason for existence. That is why we are born and that is why we are born again from above. That is why we were created and that is why we have been recreated. That is why there was a genesis at the beginning, and that is why there is a re-genesis, called regeneration. That is also why there is a church. The Christian church exists to worship God first of all. Everything else must come second or third or fourth or fifth."

We've been made in God's image. *That's who we are*, created for devotion and praise to God. Worship is the hub of human life because God is the Center. "The fear of the Lord," we've heard again and again, "is the beginning of wisdom." Anything less is god-less. "One of the greatest tragedies that we find," wrote Tozer, "even in this most enlightened of all ages, is the utter failure of millions of men and women ever to discover why they were born." Oh, the pain, never to make that discovery. Or to make it late in life. Or to know it in your heart but live like it isn't true. *So, who do you think you are?*

> *You are a chosen people, a royal priesthood, a holy nation, a people belonging to God, that you may declare the praises of him who called you out of darkness into his wonderful light.*
> 1 PETER 2:9

What Is Worship?

First, "worship" is not what most people think: Sunday (or Saturday) meetings in a religious building. Nor is worship, as it is often presumed among "full-gospel" folks, singing slow songs softly in contrast to peppy "praise" tunes. In other words, worship is neither a matter of musical style nor a programmed (or unprogrammed!) religious service, like this:

WORSHIP
Sundays 9 A.M. and 11 A.M.

Church signs imply, unintentionally, of course, that "worship" happens *only* at *those* times on *Sunday morning* and in the "worship style" of that particular congregation.

No, it's not wrong to use the word "worship" on our church marquees, but loose use of important words like worship often keeps us away from their better meanings. Jesus himself attended traditional "worship" services in the synagogue and temple from time to time, but he told a hurting woman in Samaria that, "True worshipers will worship the Father in spirit and truth, for they are the kind of worshipers the Father seeks" (Jn 4:23). So, according to Jesus, worship is primarily about "spirit and truth," *heart and life,* not a religious activity in a religious building.

Most people know that the English word "worship" means literally "to attribute worth," but worship is so much more than just telling God how wonderful he is. Oh, we need to do that, too. Singing his praises is a very good thing, and we'll talk much more about the *act* and *practice* of worship later in this book, but we can't start there. Our hearts and lives always need to be a step ahead of our mouths!

Jesus put it this way: "Love the Lord your God with all your heart and with all your soul and with all your mind and with all your strength" (Mk 12:30). True worship starts deep inside us and interfaces with everything we are and everything we do. Obviously, this also means you and I can't put God in one box and our relationships in another, as Jesus reminds us in the other half of the Great Commandment: "Love your neighbor as yourself."

How can we say we love God, whom we haven't seen, when

we're not loving all the people right there in front of our face (see 1 Jn 4:20)? Jesus even said that our singing in church hurts God's ears if things aren't right between us and somebody else: "Therefore, if you are offering your gift at the altar and there remember that your brother has something against you, leave your gift there in front of the altar. First go and be reconciled to your brother; then come and offer your gift" (Mt 5:23-24).

Worship draws a circle around everything about us, so attributing worth to God means treasuring his Word, too. To "worship" God without taking seriously what he has to say is, well, a religious joke. Look at this:

> *Love the Lord your God with all your heart and with all your soul and with all your strength. [Worship like this means that] ... these commandments that I give you today are to be upon your hearts. Impress them on your children. Talk about them when you sit at home and when you walk along the road, when you lie down and when you get up.*
>
> DEUTERONOMY 6:5-7

So here's my personal definition of worship: *Worship is encountering God, knowing and experiencing who he is, giving thanks and praise for what he has done, loving the people he loves, and daily doing what he says.* I think this is what the apostle Paul is teaching us in Romans 12:1-2: "Therefore, I urge you, brothers, in view of God's mercy, to offer your bodies as living sacrifices, holy and pleasing to God—this is your spiritual act of worship. Do not conform any longer to the pattern of this world, but be transformed by the renewing of your mind."

Worship Starts With God

Worship is loving God and living his Word, but I can't empha-
size enough that worship is not a yoke of human effort to get
religion right and pry some blessing out of heaven. The apostle
John wrote, "This is how we know that we love the children of
God: by loving God and carrying out his commands. This is
love for God: to obey his commands. And [notice this] his
commands are not burdensome" (1 Jn 5:2-3).

I'm a grace man. For me, *everything* is grace-based. The core
message of the Christian faith, unlike that of every other religion
in the world, bar none, is that God has taken the initiative to
save us. "Religion" is righteousness from us, but "in the gospel
a righteousness *from God* is revealed, a righteousness that is by
faith from first to last, just as it is written: 'The righteous will live
by faith'" (Rom 1:17).

So, ultimately, it's not up to us to find God, it's up to God to
find us. In fact, we couldn't find God if we tried! "We all, like
sheep, have gone astray, each of us has turned to his own way;
and the Lord has laid on him [Jesus Christ] the iniquity of us all"
(Is 53:6). Grace is not God's good help along the road of life,
it's his radical intervention in our helplessness. Worship is not a
catalyst of grace, it's a response to God's gloriously free gift.

Years ago I heard popular Bible teacher Bob Mumford talk
about how people like to say, "I found the Lord!" Can't you
just imagine God wrestling someone to the ground, putting his
divine knee in the guy's chest, and holding him by the throat?
I'm speaking figuratively, of course. Yet God does have to do
extraordinary things to get our attention.

So there's that dude, lying there on the ground, ribs popping
under the knee of God, and he cries out, "I found you, Lord!"

Yeah, right! You found God? I didn't know God was lost! I thought we were, which is why Jesus came both to *seek* and to save the *lost* (see Lk 19:10). God does just about everything he can to get our attention, because we are not naturally cooperative with what God wants to do in us. The human heart is bent away from God. The human heart is just plain bent!

Oh, I know some of you are thinking, "But doesn't the Bible tell us to seek God, to seek his kingdom, seek and you will find? Things like that?" Yes, it certainly does, and we definitely have a responsibility in that regard, but amazing grace is God seeking us, not the other way around. And he keeps after us, even after we're saved.

But doesn't the Bible say, "God helps those who help themselves?" *No!* That's not in the Bible, although according to national surveys, a huge proportion of people, including many born-again Christians, think it is. God doesn't meet us halfway. He intervenes and transforms us at the point of our greatest helplessness, just as we are, without one single plea.

Sinking Sand

Hey, if God rewards good works, I'm there! I don't just go to church. I am church! I've been the senior pastor of a "successful" church for twenty years, and I'm there three times a week. I have two seminary degrees. Yet I can't ever shake this unsettled feeling that if my relationship with God depended on me and my spiritual effort, I wouldn't be up to the task. I just wouldn't make it. Maybe you're different, but I have no confidence in myself. I can, though, do all things through Christ who strengthens me.

The apostle Paul pretty much felt the same way: "If anyone

else thinks he has reasons to put confidence in the flesh [not sins, but good works on our own, apart from Christ working in us], I have more: circumcised on the eighth day, of the people of Israel, of the tribe of Benjamin, a Hebrew of Hebrews; in regard to the law, a Pharisee; as for zeal, persecuting the church; as for legalistic righteousness, faultless. But whatever was to my profit I now consider loss for the sake of Christ."

"What is more," Paul adds, "I consider everything a loss compared to the surpassing greatness of knowing Christ Jesus my Lord, for whose sake I have lost all things [that would be everything Paul worked so hard on in order to create his own identity, including his very good religion]. I consider them rubbish ["dog droppings" in the Greek], that I may gain Christ and be found in him, not having a righteousness of my own that comes from the law, but that which is through faith in Christ—the righteousness that comes from God and is by faith" (Phil 3:4-9).

Paul gives me even more hope when he admits, "The Spirit helps us in our weakness [when we can't help ourselves]. We do not know what we ought to pray for, but the Spirit himself intercedes for us with groans that words cannot express.... [And that's why, in the end, we can be confident that] in all things God works for the good of those who love him, who have been called according to his purpose" (Rom 8:26, 28).

As the great historic worship hymn reminds us,

My hope is built on nothing less
    than Jesus' blood and righteousness.
I dare not trust the sweetest frame,
    but wholly lean on Jesus' name.
On Christ, the solid rock, I stand.
    All other ground is sinking sand.

Now Would Be a Good Time

My uncle, after many years of religious questions, had a dramatic encounter with Jesus in the middle of the night. "There he was," my uncle told me, "standing at the foot of my bed, asking me when I was going to become a Christian. I thought to myself, 'This is a good time.'"

How can you say no in a moment like that?!

Many years later, my uncle still cries when he tells the story. I retell it with a slice of humor (God have mercy), but its underlying message is clear: God initiates relationship with us, both *generally*, in the work of his Son on the Cross for the whole world, and *individually*, in the unique way he draws each of us gently to himself. Or maybe not so gently. The Greek text of John 6:44 could be translated, "No one comes to me unless the father who sent me *drags* him."

God "dragged" Saul, the bad killer-man on his way from Jerusalem to round up a few more Christians in Damascus. Yet God had other plans, and Jesus appeared to Saul in a blinding flash of light right there in the middle of the road. Falling to the ground, Saul heard the voice of the Lord (I'm paraphrasing): "I've been poking around in your life for a long time now, Saul. When are you going to get the message?" Without hesitation, Saul said, "I get it, Lord, I get it!"

Well, actually, Saul said nothing as he staggered blindly into his new future. Years later, Saul, now Paul, testified, "I was not disobedient to the vision from heaven" (see Acts 26:12-19). He got it. As well-known worship leader Ron Kenoly has said, "We allow ourselves to be found by the Lord."

You have your own story to tell, I'm sure, of how God got your attention. The lesson here is that *worship doesn't just focus on God, it starts with God.* It's not about what *you* do in a church service or how you do it to get a response from God. It's about who God is and what God does and our response to that. Whatever we think about worship, however we think it should be done, worship that's not rooted in the freedom of grace is not true worship.

God Loves to Love Us

Worship, then, is certainly not just ritual. It's God's enjoyment of us and our enjoyment of him. One of my many Greek language resources states that the basic meaning of the Greek word for "worship" is "to come towards to kiss (the hand), and it denotes both the act of prostrating oneself in worship and the corresponding inward attitude of reverence and humility."[1]

Worship is deep personal relationship and intimacy with God. He loves us, the Bible reminds us many times, as a father loves his children, even as a husband loves his wife. He loves us, he knows us, and he wants us to know him, but not in the sense that he wants us just to know *about* him. The word "know" is used much differently in both Hebrew and Greek than it is in English. When you and I say we "know" something, it's almost always in the sense of mental information. In contrast, the book of Genesis reports without blinking that Adam "knew" Eve. And she bore him a son! Pretty personal "knowing" there, I'd say!

Now, I'm hardly suggesting that our relationship with God is sexual, but it is personal, emotional, passionate, and intimate. Paul certainly had this in his mind and heart when he wrote of his life's quest, "I want to know Christ and the power of his resurrection and the fellowship of sharing in his sufferings, becoming like him in his death.... One thing I do [there's that "one thing" again]: Forgetting what is behind and straining toward what is ahead, I press on toward the goal to win the prize for which God has called me heavenward in Christ Jesus" (Phil 3:10,13-14).

Just "One Thing" One More Time

Let me take you through Psalm 27 to show you what happens when we spend time worshiping God, gazing upon the beauty of the Lord and seeking him in his temple. *First, our God becomes a totally safe place in a terribly unsafe world:* "For in the day of trouble he will keep me safe in his dwelling; he will hide me in the shelter of his tabernacle and set me high upon a rock" (v. 5). I think that's what a lot of people are trying to say with T-shirts and bumper stickers: NO FEAR.

Second, our God becomes very personal, in an impersonal world filled with impersonal gods: "My heart says of you, 'Seek his face!' Your face, Lord, I will seek. Do not hide your face from me" (vv. 8-9). Wow, God's face! It's so personal, like when you see the faces of the ones you love, especially when you've been separated from them for a while. You want to touch that face, kiss that face!

Next time you're at the airport, watch carefully the faces of people exiting the concourse—and the faces of those who are there to greet them. Watch how they're craning their necks. Standing on their toes. Unconsciously smiling in anticipation of seeing someone they haven't seen for a while. *Unconscious they're standing there blocking the doggone exit!* And then watch the tears of joy when eyes of family and friends and lovers meet!

Or watch me light up when I see the faces of my grand-children, little Emily and Annika! Oh, just to think about them brings a smile to *my* face. In fact, I'm having the uncontrollable urge, *right now*, to dig their pictures out of my crusty wallet.

Ah, there they are, the little honeys! Just to see their faces!

Look at that verse again: "My heart says of you, 'Seek his face!' Your face, Lord, I will seek. Do not hide your face from me."

Third, when God is the center of our lives he makes sure that everything in our lives comes together: "Teach me your way, O Lord; lead me in a straight path ..." (v. 11). Best-selling Christian author Gordon MacDonald hits on this when he writes, "If my private [personal] world is in order, it will be because I regularly choose to enlarge the spiritual center of my life." It sounds like there's just "one thing" he desires, too.

Fourth, our God protects us in our dangerous world: "Teach me your way, O Lord; lead me in a straight path because of my oppressors. Do not turn me over to the desire of my foes, for false witnesses rise up against me, breathing out violence. I am still confident of this: I will see the goodness of the Lord in the land of the living" (vv. 11-13).

Finally, when we're blue in the face with worshiping and seek-ing God, and nothing seems to be changing in our difficult cir-cumstances, what then? "Wait for the Lord; be strong and take heart and wait for the Lord" (v. 14). In other words, just keep spending time with God. What other choice is there? God is even bigger than the delay, and those "who hope in the Lord will renew their strength. They will soar on wings like eagles; they will run and not grow weary, they will walk and not be faint" (Is 40:31).

TWO

BEHOLD YOUR GOD!

*Before the Christian Church goes into eclipse anywhere ... she
simply gets a wrong answer to the question, "What is God
like?"*

A.W. Tozer

I'm hardly an auto mechanic, but I did replace the motor
mounts on my '66 Mustang convertible. There's only one
problem: I raised the engine by putting the jack on the oil pan.
Oh well, no one will ever see *that* dent.

Clueless. People are just clueless.

What's worse is that people don't know they're clueless, and
most of the time, they'd prefer you not to point it out. They
might even get angry if you try to help them, as if it's your fault
because you know something they don't.

This is why television programs like *America's Funniest
Home Videos* are so popular. It's really kind of sad, because we
love to laugh our brains out at clueless people. *Candid Camera*
has been on the air for decades, preying on unsuspecting human
beings. The lesson, of course, is that what we don't know is
vastly greater than what we do know. Our ignorance is
appalling, but we don't even know we're ignorant, which can
be downright dangerous.

I'm sure you've seen the noble attempt of one of America's
largest breweries to get people to "drink responsibly." "Think

when you drink," they remind us. I find that amusing in a sick sort of way, because when people drink, thinking pretty much comes to a screeching halt.

The apostle Paul, who was arguably as knowledgeable as any human being, was willing to confess, "The man who thinks he knows something does not yet know as he ought to know. But the man who loves God is known by God" (1 Cor 8:2-3).

Wisdom is humble awareness that what you know is only a fraction of what can be known. Pride is thinking you know it all, or at least a lot more than the other guy. Pride refuses to allow anyone else to challenge your thinking. Pride is ignorance.

Clueless About God

You can probably guess where I'm going with this: *Way too often we're clueless about God.* In the last chapter I asked, "So who do we think we are?" Or, more specifically, "Why are we here? What's the meaning and purpose of human life?" The simple answer is "to glorify God and enjoy him forever."

Tell me, though, do you do that? Do I do that? Well, sometimes. We know what we *should* believe about God and his Word. We know that sometimes it's even a matter of life and death, heaven and hell, but most of the time we're, well, clueless. And, practically speaking, godless.

Yet the problem goes deeper still. When we do get around to thinking about God and inviting him into every little thing in our lives, who is the God we're thinking about? How do we know what he's like? Dare I say that thinking wrong things about God may be even more dangerous than not thinking about God at all? In his classic work, *The Knowledge of the Holy*,

A.W. Tozer's first chapter is titled, "Why We Must Think Rightly About God." What he writes in the excerpt below has had a profound impact on my life. I've read it again and again over the past twenty-five years:

> What comes to our minds when we think about God is the most important thing about us. The history of mankind will probably show that no people has ever risen above its religion, and mankind's spiritual history will positively demonstrate that no religion has ever been greater than its idea of God. Worship is pure or base as the worshiper entertains high or low thoughts of God....
>
> Wrong thoughts about God are not only the fountain from which the polluted waters of idolatry flow; they are themselves idolatrous. The idolater simply imagines things about God and acts as if they were true....
>
> Before the Christian Church goes into eclipse anywhere there must first be a corrupting of her simple basic theology. She simply gets a wrong answer to the question, "What is God like?"

What Is God Like?

Early one morning, jogging along one of the many irrigation waterways coursing through Phoenix, I was meditating on the central question of this book: What is worship? I felt like I heard the voice of God in my heart: "You're asking the wrong question. The right question is: Who am I?"

This, I hope you know, is biblical. When God appeared to Moses in the burning bush to "call" him to ministry and send him back to Egypt, Moses wanted to know just who this God was. Sensing that a return to the land of the Pharaoh would be no vacation, Moses said to God, and I'm paraphrasing, "When I get back there, how am I supposed to explain my return? *Who are you*, burning-bush-God? *What's your name?* You know, I can't tell the Hebrews about this, me talkin' with a cactus. They'd just say I had spent too many years in the desert."

Moses wanted to know, needed to know exactly who God was, right down to his personal name. Knowing how important this was, Jesus asked his disciples, "Who do people say the Son of Man is?" And a moment later, "But what about you? Who do you say I am?" Peter got it right: "You are the Christ, the Son of the Living God." We have to get it right, too, and when we do, when we get the right answer to the right question—Who is God?—worship happens, and things happen to us:

> *"Do not come any closer," God said [to Moses]. "Take off your sandals, for the place where you are standing is holy ground." Then he said, "I am the God of your father, the God of Abraham, the God of Isaac, and the God of Jacob." At this, Moses hid his face, because he was afraid to look at God.*
>
> EXODUS 3:5-6

To Know God Is to Worship Him

Worship happens when we know God, which is why a book about worship must be a book about knowing God, not just about how to worship God. We will get to that! If this book is only about how to *do* worship, then I run the risk that readers will worship the art of worship. That happens, you know. People get more into *how* to worship than they do into God himself. It's almost as if the act of worship becomes their God. If you don't believe this, ask around in your church if anybody has ever gotten bent out of shape about how to worship. "Worship" can get really ugly when people get upset about *how* the church should or should not worship.

To know and experience God, however, is to love and worship him. People who don't know God will worship and devote themselves to something else. It's only logical: if God created us for worship, and we don't worship the God who created us, we will necessarily bow down to and serve something else. Human beings don't have a choice.

Yes, they can choose the object of their worship, but the fact that they will worship *something* is predetermined. People will eat, people will sleep, people will talk, people will think, and people will worship. Ever notice how devoted some people are to their belief that God doesn't exist? It's their religion!

Jesus used this logic, for example, when he spoke about the power of materialism. He said, "No one can *serve* two masters. Either he will hate the one and *love* the other, or he will be *devoted* to the one and despise the other. You cannot serve both God and Money."[1] Notice the terms I've highlighted: serve, love, devoted. Because of the way God created us, we will be devoted to and serve whatever we love.

So, if you love money, guess what you'll bow down to and serve? If you love your career, or your hobby, or your whatever, guess what you'll serve? Or maybe you just love you. Guess who you'll bow down to and serve: your unholy self, for which you will likely make great sacrifices (perhaps even "burning" other people) to keep the god of self happy. This is certainly why there's so much attention to the necessity of self-sacrifice in Bible.

So What Do You Think About God?

This is a book about worship, but at its heart, it's a book about God. Before I suggest some things you *should* think about God, I'd like to help you understand that what you think about spirituality may be more "American" than biblical.[2]

Nearly fifty years ago a man by the name of J.B. Phillips published *The New Testament in Modern English,* but hardly anyone knows that's the title. Mostly, people call it "the Phillips version." This same man authored a little book that became a bestseller: *Your God Is Too Small.* Published in the 1950s, it's still in print—and timeless, but times have changed. Today, I could imagine him titling his book *Your God Looks Too Much Like You.* Donald McCullough has written an exceptional book for the new century, *The Trivialization of God: The Dangerous Illusion of a Manageable Deity,* in which he presents an extraordinary analysis of why we are thinking so differently about God these days.[3]

It's not a conspiracy, where a handful of devil-filled people are trying to change our world. Yet we are being brainwashed in a massive shift and dislocation of our culture, and every one of us is vulnerable to the "values" of our brave new world, particularly rampant individualism.

"As Americans," writes McCullough, "we have had bred in our bones a thorough-going individualism. We will be tempted, therefore, to create for ourselves gods who will not threaten us with transcendence, gods who will be manifestly useful in a world of confusing voices, and gods who will conform to the contours of our individualistic desires." Out of our personal needs, we've erected temples to our own gods.

I had a strange dream. In my dream, my wife and I were

looking at model homes, and a particularly innovative home builder had designed a "chapel" of sorts into each floor plan, a neat little room set aside for whatever kind of spiritual practice might suit the owner's fancy. No need for any organized religion anymore. Just make the space comfortable for your own designer god. McCullough suggests several false gods people might like to consider:

- *The god of my cause.* My doctrine is God's doctrine. God is on my side in this family argument, this litigation, this political position, this doctrinal debate. I'm right, you're wrong, and being right is more important to me than you are.

- *The god of my understanding.* I can't trust God unless I understand God. He has to make sense to me. At the very least, he has to make sense in the context of my personal life. I know this probably isn't realistic, but somehow God has to fit into my head. It hasn't occurred to me, though, that if God fits into my head, I'm actually bigger than God.

- *The god of my experience.* Wow, that was a *great* experience, and it felt so good! It had to be God. Or an angel. You know, if something *feels* right, it *is* right. And if something *feels* bad, it must be bad. I know the Bible says that sometimes Satan disguises himself as an angel, and the Bible also makes it pretty clear that God doesn't always protect us from pain and suffering. Yet none of that really matters to me. I just know that when I feel good, that's God. If what I've experienced somehow doesn't line up with the Bible, then I'm going have to go with my experience.

- *The god of my comfort.* If life isn't good, if I'm not happy, then God must not love me. Or, if this is the way God is going to let my life unfold, then I'm not interested in God. If God is going to be into rules, or boundaries, or consequences, I don't think I can believe in that kind of God. I need a safe God.

- *The god of my success.* Every American knows that happiness is synonymous with success. I therefore know that God must want me to be successful, because he surely wants me to be happy.

Behold Your God!

OK, have I made you a little edgy? That's what happens when I go after idols. People will die to defend them. Hearing the truth is always painful for me, too, but I'd rather hear it now than later. Here's some truth about God from one of the great chapters in the Bible, Isaiah 40. Let's start in verse 9: "Behold your God!"

I was amazed to discover that the Hebrew word for "behold" is used over one thousand times in the Old Testament. Think about it. *Over one thousand times!* Why do you suppose this word is used so commonly? It's simple: we have a hard time listening! The Hebrew word translated "behold" is "an interjection demanding attention, 'look!' 'see!' ... The term emphasizes the immediacy, the here-and-now-ness, of the situation."[4]

I'm a bit of a daydreamer. Some people would say I have Attention Deficit Disorder. I've never been officially diagnosed with the problem, but it would be a handy excuse for all the times I haven't paid attention. Just ask my mother. My wife. My

kids. Or my grandfather, who called me the absent-minded professor when I was just ten.

I can still feel the sudden, searing pain in my left hand as I sat
there at my desk ... motionless ... eyes glazed ... in my fourth-
grade classroom. No, I wasn't dozing, but, man, was I deep in
thought. I can't remember what I was thinking about, but I
sure remember the pain. It was like an awakening from a coma.
Slowly rolling my head toward my throbbing hand, I saw her
out of the corner of my eye. It was my teacher! She was standing right there in front of me, striking the back of my hand with
a wooden ruler. And, lo, I heard her say in a loud voice, *"Behold,
your fourth-grade teacher!"*

Isaiah is shouting, too, trying to awaken us. God commanded
him, "You who bring good tidings to Jerusalem, lift up your
voice with a shout, lift it up, do not be afraid; say to the towns
of Judah, *'Behold your God!'"* (v. 9, KJV).

The "good tidings" are all the fantastic things God is going
to say about himself in Isaiah 40. In that moment in Jewish history, Israel was turning away from God. Black clouds of judgment[5] were billowing around the Holy City, and Isaiah was
God's man of the hour, commissioned to prophesy both judgment and hope. Something had to change, and God had to
re-reveal himself to bring about radical transformation.

They should have known better. *We should know better.* Not
once but twice in Isaiah 40 God says in holy disbelief, "Do you
not know? Have you not heard? Has it not been told you from
the beginning? Have you not understood since the earth was
founded?" It was time for God to shout his people out of their
coma, to shout some sense into them. *Behold, your God! You've
forgotten that ...*

- *Our God is more powerful than you can imagine, and his*

authority is bound only by the limits he places on himself: "See, the Sovereign Lord comes with power, and his arm rules for him.... Surely the nations are like a drop in a bucket; they are regarded as dust on the scales; he weighs the islands as though they were fine dust.... Before him all the nations are as nothing; they are regarded by him as worthless and less than nothing.... He brings princes to naught and reduces the rulers of this world to nothing" (vv. 10, 15, 17, 23).

* *Our God is bursting with blessing for those who know and obey him, and explosive with consequences for those who don't:* "See, his reward is with him, and his recompense accompanies him" (v. 10).

* *Our God is full of tender love and mercy:* "He tends his flock like a shepherd: He gathers the lambs in his arms and carries them close to his heart; he gently leads those that have young" (v. 11).

* *Our God's creative power is limitless:* "Who has measured the waters in the hollow of his hand, or with the breadth of his hand marked off the heavens? Who has held the dust of the earth in a basket, or weighed the mountains on the scales and the hills in a balance?... Lift your eyes and look to the heavens: Who created all these? He who brings out the starry host one by one, and calls them each by name. Because of his great power and mighty strength, not one of them is missing" (vv. 12, 26).

Bible scholars tell us that reference to "the stars" in this passage is not just pointing us to the magnificence of the universe. It is, in fact, an allusion to the astral deities of Babylon, which, figuratively speaking, are the principalities and powers of darkness behind all our problems. Life is a spiritual battle (see Eph 6:10-12).

- *Our God's knowledge is limitless:* "Who has understood the mind of the Lord, or instructed him as his counselor? Whom did the Lord consult to enlighten him, and who taught him the right way? Who was it that taught him knowledge or showed him the path of understanding?" (Is 40:13-14)

- *Our God's holiness is inaccessible:* "Lebanon is not sufficient for altar fires, nor its animals enough for burnt offerings" (v. 16).

- *Our God is incomparable:* "To whom, then, will you compare God? What image will you compare him to?... 'To whom will you compare me? Or who is my equal?' says the Holy One" (vv. 18, 25).

When I'm reading a book, I often skip right over the blocks of scripture text. "I know that stuff," I think to myself. Yet I don't want you just to read this book. My prayer is for you *to know and experience God. Behold, your God, and worship him!* So stop where you are, go back to the first bullet point above, and read aloud the Bible texts from Isaiah 40. Or, if you are not in a place where you can worship aloud, say them softly to yourself, closing your eyes after each point to reflect for a moment on what God is saying about himself to you.

God-Focus Refocuses Me and Changes Me Forever

Remember our starting point: wrong ideas about God. The gods we make up in our heads, gods that are no bigger than our brains, can't help us a lick. That's why, with all the new interest in spirituality, some people may be feeling more personally at peace, but are their lives changing? How about their families? Are we seeing less divorce? Or fewer social problems? As a matter of fact, as America has drifted away from God, all of the indicators of the health of our society have declined.

In striking contrast, a life of worship, one that regularly encounters the God of the Bible and obeys his Word, changes people for generations, as God has both warned and promised: "I, the Lord your God, am a jealous God, punishing the children for the sin of their fathers ... but showing love to a thousand generations of those who love me and keep my commandments."

According to Isaiah 40, then, what specifically happens when we awaken from our spiritual coma, return to the God of our fathers, and submit to his Word? Remember, I don't want you just to read this book. My prayer is that you will experience the God I'm writing about. So read the rest of this chapter, but pray it, too. Confess it aloud. Use it as a guide for personal worship.

- *As I worship you, Lord, I am confident that your presence will overpower the negative force of self-pity:* "Why do you say, O Jacob, and complain, O Israel, 'My way is hidden from the Lord; my cause is disregarded by my God'? Do you not know? Have you not heard? The Lord is the everlasting God, the Creator of the ends of the earth. He will not grow tired or weary, and his understanding no one can fathom. He gives strength to the weary and increases the power of the weak" (Is 40:27-29). Feeling like a victim is related to feeling out of control. Very simply, self-pity is unbelief, but worship reaffirms what you already know, that other people aren't really in control of your life. *God is.*

• *As I worship you, Lord, you put my problems in perspective by reminding me that what I am going through is not unique, unusual, or exceptional:* "Even youths grow tired and weary, and young men stumble and fall" (v. 30).

• *As I worship you, Lord, you renew my strength and lift me into your presence, high above my personal problems:* "Those who hope in the Lord will renew their strength. They will soar on wings like eagles; they will run and not grow weary, they will walk and not be faint" (v. 31).

The Hebrew word for "hope" ("wait" in the King James Version) means "to wait or to look for with eager expectation.... Waiting with steadfast endurance is a great expression of faith. It means enduring patiently in confident hope that God will decisively act for the salvation of his people.... Those who wait in true faith are renewed in strength so that they can continue to serve the Lord while looking for his saving work. There will come a time when all that God has promised will be realized and fulfilled. In the meantime the believer survives by means of his integrity and uprightness as he trusts in God's grace and power."[6]

Isaiah 40 stirs our faith and turns us back to God, not because it's full of motivational thoughts, but because it's the Word of

God about God. Those *who wait on the Lord* are those who keep worshiping. As they do, God will become more and more real, and they will renew their strength.

> *Do you not know? Have you not heard? Has it not been told you from the beginning? Have you not understood since the earth was founded? Behold, your God!*

And worship him.

THREE

HOLY AWE

Holy, holy, holy is the Lord Almighty;
the whole earth is full of his glory.

ISAIAH 6:3

The toy store is cavernous. A father and his little boy navigate the deep canyons of delight. Their eyes wander up the steep walls of colorful packages, kaleidoscopic towers so high they seem to disappear in cloudy mists above.

A child's paradise!

But the poor kid is buckled in, strapped to a wobbling shopping cart, while Dad is making every effort to steer the quivering wheels dead center in the aisle. He knows that a move of just inches to the right or left will put every box, every package within reaching distance of those excited, little hands.

"No, you can't have that."

"No, not that either."

"You want to see this? Here, you can look at it, but we can't open the package."

"You can look, but you can't touch."

Why do we do that to our kids? Why do we tease them with toy catalogs before Christmas, telling them they can pick *three* things, that's all? It's torture! Why can't they open a single package—

some of them under the tree for days or weeks—until that very special moment when the whole family gathers? It's torture!

Well, in fact, it's not really sadism on our part. As adults, we know Christmas will be here in the blink of eye, that life is not about having everything, that it's just fine to enjoy a few things, and *having* something is not nearly as much fun as *thinking* about having it. It's the joy of expectation and the nervous energy of anticipation that make Christmas such a delight.

That's faith! "Faith is being sure of what we hope for and certain of what we do not see" (Heb 11:1). I have to be honest. Sometimes *that* feels like torture! Why do I have to keep believing? Why can't I have it now?

Don't you get it? The fun is in going there, not just in getting there. The joy is in the journey, not just the destination. Isn't that what you tell your kids on a long family trip? *Look out the window! It's fun to be together!* And as an adult, you really mean that. My wife and I love to just "go on drives." Are we getting old, or is there really something to this?

Sure, it's great to make progress, to arrive. You can't drive twenty-four-seven. Yet in my relationship with God, because he's so awesome, there is a sense in which I will *never* arrive, and that's what keeps me going farther and higher and deeper.

The Joy of the Journey of Faith

Did you ever think about this? The Bible says, "faith, hope, and love" *abide* (See 1 Cor 13:13, RSV).

I can hear the questions: You mean faith and hope don't go away when we get to heaven? Heaven is what I have faith in, hope for. We're still going to need faith?

Yes! Because faith is expectation and anticipation that God always has more in store for us. No, our need for faith and hope is not going to end when we get to heaven, because heaven has no end.

Doesn't this just make you want to worship the God of heaven, the God of eternity? Only a God without limits is a God worthy of worship, a God "who is able to do *immeasurably more than all we ask or imagine,* according to his power that is at work within us, to whom be glory in the church and in Christ Jesus throughout all generations, for ever and ever!" (Eph 3:20-21). God is not at the end of the road, because the road to God never ends.

I want more of you, God! More of you!

To use another word picture, the purpose of eating is to fill your stomach with nutrients for your whole body. Yet that's not why I eat. I eat because I like food, and when I'm eating, I'm not thinking about how the molecules in my sour cream, salsa, and guacamole are making their way to my brain cells. I'm just loving the chips!

If I didn't get full, I'd just keep eating. Did you ever sit down to a really good noon meal and find yourself asking, "So what are we having for supper tonight?" It's one of the reasons I love life, because I get to eat all over again every day! Eating one good meal just whets your appetite for another. "Give us this day our daily bread."

Yet didn't Jesus say, "Seek and you will find; knock and the door will be opened"? Jesus surely did say these things, but when you seek God, when he opens the door and you receive your blessing, you will discover more doors for knocking on, more of God to know and receive. And, yeah, that's going to go on forever! That's Christmas 365 days a year, with every single day feeling better than the day before.

My oldest son will kill me for writing about this, but one Christmas, as I tucked him in bed, he made the terrible mistake of telling me, "You know, Dad, I didn't really get very much for Christmas this year." It makes me laugh out loud right now as I'm recalling the moment, but I didn't laugh at the time! Even the best Christmas, you see, can leave you feeling empty.

But not God. His mercies are new every morning, and there's something fresh and wonderful to discover every time we enter his presence in worship. I decided long ago that I will have to live forever, because that's how long it's going to take to get to know our infinite God! No, heaven is not going to be a dead end. Even after a few thousand years, we still won't be bored.

"Do you not know? Have you not heard? Has it not been told you from the beginning? Have you not understood since the earth was founded? *Behold, your God!*" How can we ever get enough of him? How can we ever get enough love? "There is no remedy for love but love more," wrote Henry David Thoreau.

Not Too Much Theology

People love "spirituality" but have an aversion for organized religion and doctrine. People think God is wonderful but feel theology is boring. Yet theology is simply the human heart's quest to know and understand God. The study of theology without the experience of God certainly can be tedious and dull, something for old men in musty libraries. Yet our experience of God, which is how we often think of the act of worship, must be grounded in good, solid biblical teaching—theology, if you will.

Actually, I tricked you in the first part of this chapter. I wasn't just talking about toys, Christmas, and family vacations, I was introducing you to some of the deepest teachings about God in the Bible, specifically two interrelated truths: (1) the transcendence and immanence of God, and (2) the mystery of the Trinity.

Don't be intimidated by these terms. Bear with me, now—theology is life-changing, and I am determined to make it as interesting and understandable as possible. In fact, I am praying that what you are about to read in the rest of this chapter will touch you so deeply that you won't be able to finish the next few pages without putting this book down to reflect and worship.

Immanence and Transcendence

It's really quite simple: God is both approachable (he's immanent) and unapproachable (he's transcendent). God is everywhere, and near to every one of us, but he stands outside of and apart from the time-space world he created.

Here's what the Bible says about God's *immanence*, his openness and accessibility to mere human beings: "Therefore, brothers, since we have confidence to enter the Most Holy Place by the blood of Jesus ... let us draw near to God with a sincere heart in full assurance of faith, having our hearts sprinkled to cleanse us from a guilty conscience" (Heb 10:19-22).

And here's what the Bible says about *transcendence*, how God remains forever inaccessible: "God, the blessed and only Ruler, the King of kings and Lord of lords, who alone is immortal and who lives in unapproachable light, whom no one has seen or can see. To him be honor and might forever. Amen" (1 Tm 6:15-16).

God is our friend. He invites us into his presence. Yet don't fool yourself. Grace doesn't mean that God is some good buddy in the sky. Isaiah certainly didn't get this impression when God appeared to him:

> *And they were calling to one another: "Holy, holy, holy is the Lord Almighty; the whole earth is full of his glory." At the sound of their voices the doorposts and thresholds shook and the temple was filled with smoke. "Woe to me!" I cried. "I am ruined! For I am a man of unclean lips, and I live among a people of unclean lips, and my eyes have seen the King, the Lord Almighty."*
>
> ISAIAH 6:3-5

More than anything, the transcendent awesomeness of God inspires worship, but his immanence, specifically his incarnation in the Person of his Son, Jesus Christ, allows us to worship.

Worship is entering God's presence, approaching him as a welcoming friend, but that's only possible because of what God has done in Christ. Look again at Hebrews 10:19, 22: "Therefore, brothers, since we have confidence to enter the Most Holy Place by the blood of Jesus, let us draw near to God with a sincere heart in full assurance of faith."

My story about the child in the toy store can help us understand how God is both immanent and transcendent: you can touch what's in your reach, and you can even take a few things home (immanence). You can't have it all, though, because if you did, you wouldn't know what to do with it, and besides, they never stop putting new stuff in the store to keep you coming back for more (transcendence). God's nearness keeps us satisfied with daily packages of blessing, but God will forever remain unapproachably transcendent, keeping us in a perpetual state of holy dissatisfaction, wild expectation, and deep reverence.

For centuries, believers have fallen on their faces before the incomprehensible God of Scripture. His magnificent mystery makes our heads spin, our hearts fill with wonder and awe, and our knees bend in worship: "Like the appearance of a rainbow in the clouds on a rainy day, so was the radiance around him. This was the appearance of the likeness of the glory of the Lord. When I saw it, *I fell facedown*" (Ez 1:28).

God in Three Persons

In the last chapter I talked about the fact that many people are generally clueless about life and God, but if there's anything about the God of the Bible that leaves people *really* clueless, it's the Trinity. Yet, probing the mystery of the Triune God is much like pondering his transcendence. Going deep into the Trinity is a catalyst for worship and adoration. Perhaps that's why one of the best known and most worshipful hymns of the Christian faith, sung in nearly every church setting, Protestant and Catholic, charismatic and noncharismatic, is:

Holy, holy, holy, Lord God Almighty,
Early in the morning our song shall rise to thee!
Holy, holy, holy, Merciful and Mighty,
God in three Persons, blessed Trinity.

Or this one:

Praise God from whom all blessings flow,
Praise him all creatures here below,
Praise him above, ye heavenly hosts,
Praise Father, Son, and Holy Ghost.

I just can't write about worship without writing about God, and how could I possibly write about God and say nothing about the Trinity? I know some of you may be thinking, "Oh no, not more doctrine! I could hardly get past immanent and transcendent."

It's troubling to me that in most really good churches, even in churches known for their wonderful worship, you'll hardly ever hear teaching on the Trinity, as if it were some ancient theological idea, an irrelevant technicality in the doctrine of the Christian God. Yes, I'd love to give you three easy steps to get the most out of God in thirty minutes of music on Sunday, but the God of the Bible is not the genie in the bottle.

Think about it. When was the last time you heard a good sermon about the Trinity, a teaching that helped you understand the mystery of the Godhead? Or, if you're a pastor or Bible teacher, what do you know about this fundamental element of the God we worship, and have you called people to worship Father, Son, and Holy Ghost? Roderick T. Leupp writes in his wonderful book, *Knowing the Name of God,*

> For most Christians, the Trinity is the great unknown. The Trinity, to use a familiar equation, is viewed as a riddle wrapped up inside a puzzle and buried in an enigma. A riddle, for how can any entity be at the same time multiple (three) yet singular (one)? A puzzle, for the Trinity is so clearly contrary to any rational thought as not to warrant a second thought from sensible people. An enigma, for even if the Trinity could be understood, of what practical value, even what religious value, would it have for ordinary people?

The Christian tradition describes the Trinity in another

word—pure, deep, undefiled *mystery*. Pure mystery, because the mystery derives from God and in fact is God. Deep mystery, because this mystery shines in its own light and is its own depth. Undefiled mystery, because nothing can be added to or subtracted from it.

A.W. Tozer, a man whom we met earlier in the book, wrote about the Trinity,

> Our sincerest effort to grasp the incomprehensible mystery of the Trinity must remain forever futile, and only by deepest reverence can it be saved from actual presumption.... We cover our deepest ignorance with words, but we are ashamed to wonder, we are afraid to whisper "mystery." ... What God declares [about himself] the believing heart confesses without the need of further proof. Indeed, to seek proof is to admit doubt, and to obtain proof is to render faith unnecessary.... The doctrine of the Trinity is truth for the heart.... Love and faith are at home in the mystery of the Godhead. *Let reason kneel in reverence outside.*[1]

Behold, your God!
Holy, holy, holy, blessed Three Persons of the Trinity.
Amazing love, how can it be, that you, my God, would die for me? I worship and adore you, mysterious and incomprehensible God, as distant as the span of the universe, so close you are the air I breathe.

Worship the Trinity!

Although the word "Trinity" does not appear in the Bible, it is a term nearly as old as the Bible. For most of Christian history, the church has used the word "Trinity" to designate the one God self-revealed in Scripture as Father, Son, and Holy Spirit. The Christian doctrine of the Trinity is a belief that God is one in being, or essence, who exists eternally in three distinct, coequal "Persons." On the one hand, these "Persons" are not three gods, nor are they three parts or "modes" of God, but together as One they are equally and forever One God.

Yes, *they* are *One*.

You may be surprised to know that the doctrine of the Trinity did not come out of a study of the nature of God, per se. It grew out of many discussions and arguments in the early church about the nature of Jesus Christ. Everyone agreed there was a God in heaven and that Jesus was his Son, but who was Jesus, really? Was he an extraordinary, divinely inspired human being? Or was he, is he, fully *God*?

They decided, of course, that Jesus was the latter. *Jesus is Lord,* not only in the sense that he rules over all, but also in the sense that he is, in the nature of his being, God. Jesus was not divine, but Deity. Not just godly, but God. Not *a* god, but *the* God. Not part of God, but God himself. Deity in human form. *God made flesh.*

Yet this answer, that Jesus is fully God, led to other questions, like: If Jesus was God and is God, who is "the Father God" Jesus talked about and prayed to? Was that a different God? No, the Father is God, too, the early Christians decided. But wait, if the Father is God and Jesus is God, are there two Gods? No again! Jesus and the Father—and the Holy Spirit as well—are *each* God and *all* God. Three Persons, One God.

If Jesus Is God, Then God Is Trinity

Therefore, to believe in the Trinity as Christians have understood it for most of church history is to believe that Jesus is God. Furthermore, to believe that Jesus is God is to believe in the Trinity. The doctrines are mutually inclusive. You cannot believe the one without believing the other, and anyone who does not believe in the Trinity does not really believe Jesus is God.

Yes, it's a fact: Wherever you find people who do not teach the traditional doctrine of the Trinity, like Mormons or Jehovah's Witnesses, you will find people who have a lesser view of Christ. In every case, they don't believe that Jesus was and is *fully* God. For them, Jesus is godly, godlike, divine, a god, but not God himself.[2] The doctrine of the Trinity, then, is not just about who God is. It starts with who Jesus Christ is: fully man and fully God, and if Jesus is God, and the Father is God, and there's only one God, then Jesus and the Father (and the Spirit) must be unique "Persons" in the Godhead.

My logic here shows how the historic Christian understanding of the Trinity grows out of a blending of different things the Bible teaches us about the nature of God and his works in creation and salvation. The Bible teaches (1) both the immanence and the transcendence of God, and (2) both the oneness of God and the distinctions or Persons within the Godhead.

For example, in the Old Testament, in a time in history when virtually everyone believed in many gods, the God of the Hebrews revealed himself as the one and only: "Hear, O Israel: The Lord our God, the Lord is one" (Dt 6:4). Yet, amazingly, the Hebrew word for God, *elohim,* is plural, and means, literally, "gods"! How could that be? Christians believe that this plural word for God in the Hebrew Scriptures is a veiled reference to the Trinity.

Traces of the Trinity

Look at all the traces of the Trinity in the many plural terms used in the Creation account in Genesis 1:1-3 and 26: "In the beginning *God* [*elohim,* "the gods"] created the heavens and the earth.... And *God* [*elohim,* "the gods"] said, "Let there be light," and there was light.... Then *God* [*elohim,* "the gods"] said, "Let *us* [plural] make man in *our* [plural] image, in *our* [plural] likeness" (Gn 1:1, 3, 26).

The apostle John replays Genesis 1 and finds Jesus. He introduces his story of the Christ by using a phrase familiar to his Jewish readers: "*In the beginning....*" Yes, right there on the first day of Creation "was the Word [Jesus Christ], and the Word was with God [Jesus is separate from the Father], and the Word was God [Jesus is God]. He was with God [separate from the Father] in the beginning [at the time of Creation].... In him was life, and that life was the light of men. [God said, "Let there be light," but his Son Jesus is the true light.] The light shines in the darkness"(Jn 1:1-5).

Logically Impossible

This is logically impossible! Think about it: "the Word was with God, and the Word was God." That's like saying, "I am with my wife, and I am my wife." Strange? No, it's just another place where we must believe something about God that we can't explain: Jesus is with God and Jesus is God. Not strange, but a mystery so profound I've come to believe the doctrine of the Trinity *must* be true, *must* be the only proper "explanation" of the nature of God, because human beings couldn't come up a with religious idea nobody can explain![3] As A.W. Tozer wrote, "Such a truth had to be revealed; no one could have imagined it."

"So what?" you might ask. "I'm still not sure how all this theologizing can lead me into deeper worship." Well, ponder this, then: When the Bible says, "For God so loved the world that he gave his one and only Son," underlying this free gift to us was a decision among the three Persons of the Godhead to disrupt their eternal relationship with one another. Our sin tore apart the eternal, Triune Being of the Godhead, and God in his love let it happen. Ever said about some terrible thing, "This is just tearing me apart inside"? Well, that's what happened to God when Jesus came to die. God not only sacrificed his Son, he gave up something of the eternal harmony of his Triune Being.

Yes, he loves us that much.

Just look at the arms of Jesus spread wide on the cross.

Just look at the Triune God looking so unlike himself, because something of his eternal being was ripped away when part of him entered time and space and died. It was only as Jesus was resurrected, only as the Son returned to the Father, that the Godhead once again became whole. And now, in his incomprehensible sacrifice of himself, he offers us forgiveness and healing. Like the veil in the temple the day Jesus died, God was torn apart to put us back together.

Don't tell me knowing about the Trinity is unimportant, or that it doesn't deepen my love and worship for God! Our Triune God is the utterly transcendent One who became utterly approachable when he took upon himself human flesh. This is why we worship both the God who is above and beyond, who cannot be adequately described in human language, and the One who has become one of us through the Incarnation.[4] *The exalted God of heaven is down to earth.*

So immanent, so personal:

> *For we do not have a high priest who is unable to sympathize with our weaknesses, but we have one who has been tempted in every way, just as we are—yet was without sin. Let us then approach the throne of grace with confidence, so that we may receive mercy and find grace to help us in our time of need.*
> HEBREWS 4:15-16

And so transcendent, so above and beyond, so able to do for us whatever has to be done:

> *Such a high priest meets our need—one who is holy, blameless, pure, set apart from sinners, exalted above the heavens.*
> HEBREWS 7:26

Behold, your God!
He loves us so much
he ripped himself apart
tore up Trinity
by sending his Son, the Second Person
of the Godhead
into time and space
to become the man, Christ Jesus
on the cross
to carry the sins of the world
mine
yours
out of the grave.
Our sin, my sin
raped the nature of God.
Amazing love, how can it be
that you, my transcendent God,
would come close to me
and die.
Behold, your God!

FOUR

You Had to Be There

*That which was from the beginning, which we have heard,
which we have seen with our eyes, which we have looked at
and our hands have touched—this we proclaim concerning
the Word of life. The life appeared; we have seen it.*

1 John 1:1-2

Ever been in love?

Maybe you are in love, right now.

Or maybe you used to be in love. Remember that guy your
mother just couldn't stand? Explain that, please.

My point is that you can't, because love isn't just an entry in
an encyclopedia. I could ask hundreds of people what they think
about love, take notes, assess and catalog their comments, and
write a three-hundred-page book on the meaning and experience of love, and guess what? No one who read it would really
get it until they fell in love. Then they'd start using words like
"breathless" and "speechless," and saying things like "I don't
have words to describe what I'm feeling!"

Take something as simple as a really great vacation. A cruise.
Two weeks with your family in California. Or Hawaii! Go
ahead, take lots of pictures, even videos. When you get home,
spend an evening showing the blurry, not-so-well-framed photos to your best friends. Make sure you tell them about every

little thing that was so special to you. And when they yawn, they'll plead with glazed eyes, "We really are interested." In moments like this all you can say is, "You had to be there."

I just returned from Europe last week. Having a fascination with military history, I arranged to spend several days in Normandy, France, the site of the World War II D-Day Allied invasion of the European continent. You can't imagine the flood of thoughts and emotions I felt when, visiting the American cemetery on the windy bluffs above Omaha Beach, I stood in a vast sea of ten thousand white crosses.

There I go, trying to get you to feel what I felt.

You had to be there.

What would veterans of D-Day have to tell us about those "sacred" places? What they experienced is inconceivable for those of us who were not there. Yet more than half a century after those events, many World War II vets still weep when they share their memories of the friends they lost and how those friends died. Instead of telling us, "You had to be there," they're more likely to say something like, "You can be grateful you were never there."

Experiencing God

Our experience of God can also be indescribable, unique to each individual.

In one of those "Kodak moments," a freeze-frame memory that I've cherished for thirty years, I see my wife, Marilyn, her hands lifted to God, hardly knowing I was there. Not really speaking to me or to anyone else, she sighed softly, "Oh, Jesus feels so real to me right now." She was lost in holy space, and I couldn't get her attention. Not that I wanted to. How could I interrupt her extraordinary moment with God? My wife was experiencing God, and I was experiencing the moment.

You had to be there.

Yes, it's good to know *about* God, to think *about* God as you sit in church or read the Bible or books about him, to discuss what you believe about him with friends. It's good to hear somebody else "sharing their testimony," talking about what God has done in his or her life. It's all good! Yet God not only wants us to know and love him personally, he also wants us *to experience his presence.*

Some of you, undoubtedly, resonate with what I am writing. *You've been there!* So when you hear somebody talking about *experiencing* God, you just want to shout, "Amen!" Others of you reading this book may have another response. You may be thinking to yourself, "Where is the author going with this? It makes me nervous whenever someone talks about religious *experience,* because experiences can be so subjective. Besides, I'm not a very emotional person. I'd rather make sure my faith is grounded in the objective truth of the Bible."

How can I disagree with that? That's where *my* faith starts, too, in the Scriptures, where we read about how God has revealed himself to us in the Person of his Son, Jesus Christ. My relationship with God is not primarily an experience, and I most certainly can never determine how much God loves me, or whether or not he's working in my life, based on what I am feeling. I must always subject my emotions to the objective, "propositional truth" of Scripture.[1]

Getting back to the starting point of this chapter, love, we would all agree that love is not *primarily* a feeling, either. It's a commitment, regardless of how you feel. That's why we pastors, when we do weddings, insist that couples promise to love each other "for better or for worse, for richer or for poorer, in sickness or in health, until death do us part." It's love to die for!

Love that's no deeper than feelings or sentiment, love that lasts only as long as the other person is lovable, isn't love. "Conditional love" is, in fact, an oxymoron, a contradiction in terms. Love is rooted in truth and facts and covenant, not feelings.

Yet love without feelings isn't love, either. What if I told you my wife and I have been married for thirty years (which is true), but we really don't have any feelings for one another? Never a tender touch, no passionate moments. We just live together and, yeah, we believe in love, we even believe we love each other. We talk about our love, too. We just never feel it.

You know what you'd say? You'd say our marriage was in trouble. Why? Because even though love is primarily a commitment that overrules and outlasts feelings, love without feelings isn't really love. God has created us with a wealth and depth of emotions, and a great deal of life is existential. It's about what we experience.

Yes, I'm using the word "existential" deliberately, not in its full philosophical sense (for you more informed readers), but in its practical one. One dictionary indicates that this term refers to "the experience of existence." Human beings don't just exist; they *experience* existence. It's existential to say, "You had to be there," or, "Been there, done that."

Feeling his Presence?

Not too many years ago, my oldest son, David, was student body chaplain at a very large and prominent Christian university. An excellent place of higher education with a deep commitment to the Bible, this wonderful institution was, however, not known for "revival." Well, it happened. People started *experiencing* things—and getting emotional. Others got angry (not emotional, of course) about their friends getting emotional.

Many said the "revival" was, well, "just emotions," based on the pervasive presumption that Christians should not get emotional about their faith, and that if they do, it's likely to be spiritually dangerous. For these people, whatever God actually might have been doing in people's lives during that season of revival was dumped into the trash bin of "emotionalism."

Let me help you with this: emotional-*ism*, where people live for and out of their emotional experiences, can certainly be a real and serious problem. Emotionalism is not "biblical." Yet to dismiss genuine emotional experiences with God as emotionalism isn't "biblical" either! It is, in fact, cultural. You see, white North American and northern European peoples are not exactly known for their outbursts of emotion, except at an English soccer game or the World Series (see chapter 1!). I once heard the story of a farmer in Minnesota who loved his wife so much that he almost told her! Yeah, that would be my family, at times. A little too cold from the north country.

Yet the Bible was not written in Scandinavia. It was written in the warmth of Middle Eastern and Mediterranean culture, and you can't read Scripture without "feeling" it, because the writers of the Bible didn't just record good and necessary religious principles. No, they wrote about what they *felt*, too. Just read the Psalms and look for exclamation marks! Feel the pain, experience the anger, watch the joyful, emotional praise. Even the Great Commandment affirms our emotional experience of God: "Love the Lord your God with all your heart, and with all your soul, and with all your mind" (Mt 22:37).

The *Shekinah*, God's Special Presence

Let's take this a step further. The Bible not only validates emotional expressions of worship and praise for God, it teaches something else with which we are surprisingly unfamiliar in "Western" Christianity: the special presence of God. To say it in a way that will really get your attention: *God is not everywhere.*

No, I'm not denying one of the fundamental elements of the nature of God revealed in Scripture, that God is omnipresent. Yet, surprisingly, that's not all God is. It is amazingly clear throughout the Bible that God, paradoxically, is *both* omnipresent *and* specially present. On one level God is everywhere all at the same time, even in the belly of a fish at the bottom of the sea. Ask Jonah. God's *general* presence is pervasive. God is omnipresent, everywhere present.[2]

Yet God is close at hand, too. He is personal, immanent, having revealed himself in his Son, the Second Person of the Trinity made flesh in the man, Christ Jesus. God is also personally and uniquely present in specific times and places. The Hebrews had a term for this, the *shekinah*, which they used to refer to the *special* or manifested presence of God seen and experienced in the Old Testament:

- A radiant mist by day and a fire by night as Jahweh led the Hebrews through the wilderness of Sinai (see Ex 13:21-22).

- The impenetrable and dreadful cloud of glory hovering over the Ark of the Covenant, veiled in the Holy of Holies behind the heavy shroud in the tabernacle of David and later in the temple of Solomon (see 1 Kgs 8:10-11).

- An ecstatic experience as the Spirit of God fell on the ancient prophets, priests, and kings (see, for example, Jgs 14:6; 1 Sm 19:23-24; Ex 3:12-15).

For the Hebrews who knew the omnipotent, omniscient, and omnipresent Jahweh, it was this *special* presence, "the glory of God," that sustained them. As *shekinah* was the life of Israel, *Ichabod* was its death. You've heard of him, haven't you? No, not the Crane character in the cartoon, but the grandson of the wicked, self-indulgent high priest of Israel, Eli, in the book of 1 Samuel.

Not long before the crowning of Israel's first king, Saul, the people of God were fighting a losing battle with the Philistines. Thinking that the ark of the covenant was a kind of good luck weapon for their army, the Israelites dragged the holy artifact onto the field of battle only to be defeated by the Philistines, who carried away the ark of God as spoils of war.

When news of the defeat reached the families of the slain, Eli, whose two sons were killed, fell from his chair and died. Meanwhile, his daughter-in-law collapsed in premature labor, bearing a son to a father he would never know. "She named the boy Ichabod, saying, 'The glory has departed from Israel'—because of the capture of the ark of God and the deaths of her father-in-law and her husband. She said, 'The glory has departed from Israel, for the ark of God has been captured'" (1 Sm 4:21-22).

Gone! The special presence of God, gone!

You may be asking, "But isn't God everywhere?" Yes, he is! But not his *special* presence. Even in the New Testament, Jesus himself warned the church in Ephesus, "Yet I hold this against you: You have forsaken your first love. Remember the height from which you have fallen! Repent and do the things you did at first. If you do not repent, I will come to you and remove your lampstand from its place" (Rv 2:4-5). The One who walked among the seven lampstands (symbols of the seven churches of Asia Minor), gracing those churches with his personal touch and blessing, threatened to set one of those churches aside, out of the range of his special presence.

Gone! The *special* presence of God, gone! *Ichabod!*

Worship and the Special Presence of God

What does this have to do with worship? In both the Old and New Testaments, worship is not merely singing songs about God, or even to God. Worship is intended to be an experience of the *shekinah*, an encounter with the glory of God, a powerful moment in his *special* presence. My friend Myles Munroe says in his book *The Purpose and Power of Praise and Worship* that "God's goal throughout history has been to get man back into his presence." Plain and simple, that's why we worship!

This is certainly the thrust of many places in the Old Testament where the place-name Zion, the highest point in Jerusalem, also called "the mountain of God," is used almost as a synonym for God's special, manifested presence. Zion was the dwelling place of God, and to go up to Zion was to go where God was. Think about it: why would that be necessary if God is everywhere? Because he is and he isn't! It was only in Zion that people could encounter and experience the safety and power of God's personal, life-changing presence and glory.

You had to go there.

So deeply was this idea of God-in-Zion buried in the soul of

Israel that it became a point of serious contention with their half-brothers, the Samaritans. The woman at the well Jesus met one day in Samaria asked him about this very matter: "Our fathers worshiped on this mountain, but you Jews claim that the place where we must worship is in Jerusalem" (Jn 4:20).

Jesus answered her, "Believe me, woman, a time is coming when you will worship the Father neither on this mountain nor in Jerusalem. You Samaritans worship what you do not know; we worship what we do know, for salvation is from the Jews [that is, technically speaking, Mount Zion in Jerusalem was the correct place to worship]" (Jn 4:21-22).

Jesus is telling us here that God's special presence is no longer confined to a specific geographical location, Zion. Yet the glory of God, the *shekinah*, is still accessible. We can still experience his special presence. How? In the act of worship: "Yet a time is coming and has now come when the true worshipers will worship the Father in spirit and truth, for they are the kind of worshipers the Father seeks. God is spirit, and his worshipers must worship in spirit and in truth" (Jn 4:23-24).

Imagine, God is looking for worshipers whose hearts are open ("in spirit") and who have submitted their mind, will, and emotions to the Word of God ("in truth"). No longer are we expected to go up to Zion. Instead, Zion comes to us when we worship, as the psalmist declares of Jahweh, "You are the praise of Israel" (Ps 22:3). God is looking for worship, worship invites God's presence, and worship is where we encounter and experience the *shekinah*.

To enter worship is to enter the presence of God. The gates of Zion are even named "Praise" (Is 60:18), and maybe that's why God has such a fondness for them: "The Lord loves the gates of Zion more than all the dwellings of Jacob" (Ps 87:2).

So it's no surprise that we are commanded to "enter his gates with thanksgiving and his courts with praise" (Ps 100:4). Worship, then, is more than a Sunday church service. It's more than singing hymns or choruses, or even singing them passionately.

Worship is the entry point into the special presence of God. Worship is the experience of God and an encounter with God.

If you haven't been there, you need to go there!

FIVE

Transformation

True worshipers take steps of obedience.
True worshipers say and do.

Bob Fitts

And we ... are being transformed into his likeness with ever-increasing glory, which comes from the Lord, who is the Spirit.
2 CORINTHIANS 3:18

Change is not a four-letter word!"

I said that over and over to our congregation during a time of transition in our church. Why? It's common knowledge that it's uncommon for church people to accept change.

In fact, resistance to change isn't just a church problem. People *everywhere* hate to change. How do people where you work, for example, respond to changes in the org chart, to policy revisions, or to a new job description? How do they react to relocating desks and office spaces? How about when someone turns down the A/C? Or, try telling your teenager to clean her room.

Yeow! Any of these things could be right up there with declaring war! Yet changes in life are inevitable. As best-selling Christian author Rick Warren likes to say, "All living things grow," to which I add, "No change, no growth." To grow is to change. It's another one of those enigmas of life: God never changes, but change is constant in the world he created.

True, change just to be different may be change for the wrong reason and change for nothing, and there are certain elements of life that must *never* change, like the teaching of the Bible. Even the church, intended by God to be an agent of change, is also expected by God to hold fast and stand firm as "the pillar and foundation of the truth" (1 Tm 3:15).

Changing the essentials of our faith is entirely unacceptable, and "compromise" is a good word for a bad kind of change. "Transformation," on the other hand, is a term for the good kind of change. In one of the best-known passages in the New Testament, Paul writes, "Do not conform any longer to the pattern of this world, *but be transformed* by the renewing of your mind" (Rom 12:2). This verse, it's quite clear, is teaching that change begins in the mind, when we start thinking differently about ourselves, our lives, and others. One of the pastors on my staff, Andy Jackson, refers to this as cognitive transformation.

Changing Your *Nous*

I'm not fond of religious-sounding words, like "repent," because they carry centuries of baggage. Most often, though, people simply have no idea what they mean. No, "repent" does not mean "have a life-changing experience with God," although that certainly is involved. Instead, the Greek term for "repentance," *metanoia,* simply means "mind change."[1] To repent is to change the way you think about God and yourself, and when that happens, everything else in your life will change.

To expand this a bit, the landmark reference on New Testament Greek words, *Theological Dictionary of the New Testament*, edited by Gerhard Kittel, tells us that repentance means "to change one's *nous*, that is, opinion, feelings, purpose." And the *nous*? What's that? It's your "inner sense directed toward a certain object," what you perceive to be true, your "mode of thought." Shades of meaning in the Greek term *nous* include mind, insight, understanding, judgment, and meaning. When you "repent," you change all of these things, or to use Paul's language, you are transformed, that is, *radically changed*,[2] by the renewing of your mind. And that happens when you hear the Word of God.

Every Christian, it seems, has a pretty good idea about this, that people have to repent, that we have to change the way we think, and when we change the way we think, we change. It's also common knowledge that none of this can happen without preaching and teaching the Bible. The Word of God transforms us.

Is Reading the Bible Enough?

Here I go again, turning over those apple carts of common thinking. I've come to a deep conviction that teaching and studying the Bible are not, in themselves, enough to change people. A year or so ago, George Barna reported in his research that sermons change people some but not much, certainly far less than the people in our pulpits and pews assume (God have mercy on all of us preachers).

Certainly, truth and its proclamation are central to the mission of the church, but the church is not just a teaching institution.

The church is a community in which people are to be committed to one another, to encourage one another, and to live out their lives in accountable relationships: "And let us consider how we may spur one another on toward love and good deeds. Let us not give up meeting together, as some are in the habit of doing, but let us encourage one another—and all the more as you see the Day approaching" (Heb 10:24-25).

Barna's research has confirmed that community is essential to the transformation of people's lives. Teaching people the truth (preaching) is necessary, he found, but real change occurs when a person faces a challenge or crisis *and* that individual has significant, accountable relationships with people who walk him or her through it. Indeed, the practice of our faith is impossible without other people around us, both to test our love, sometimes severely, and to guide us through difficult times.

I love the Bible, and I'm known as a teaching pastor. Remarkably, I've been at the same church for twenty years, which translates into about a thousand sermons. Writing messages and preaching them has had no little effect on my own life, as I've had to hear my preaching three times every week (we do three identical services each weekend), and my wife, for my edification, even reminds me from time to time what she has heard me say. I've also been to multiple conferences, listened to many teaching cassettes, and read countless books. It's all helped!

Yet the most significant transformations in my life have been the consequence of the application of the Word of God in times of considerable difficulty and pain. As I've heard said, change happens when the pain caused by change seems to be less than the pain caused by not changing. In other words, change occurs when it becomes more painful to stay the same than it is to change! "Various trials" and a couple of "dark nights" for my soul have definitely produced "perseverance" and "character" (see Jas 1:2-4), but in the same breath I have to credit my survival and growth to the correction, encouragement, and support of godly family and friends.

Just this last year, I was really struggling with my "job." Twenty years in the same church, four huge capital stewardship programs in fifteen years, staff and board conflict. I was thinking that maybe my restlessness and discontent were indicators of God moving me on, but before I made any decision, I called together a half dozen of my closest friends and colleagues to spend an evening with me and my wife, Marilyn, to speak truth into our lives.

The results of that night together have been extraordinary. I have found a new dimension of peace in my life and ministry, and renewed strength to continue to serve at Word of Grace. *I could not and cannot sort through my feelings, know the will of God for my life, or make life decisions without significant personal relationships in the body of Christ.*

The Game of Life

It's like learning a new game. You know, when you're with family or friends, and they reach into the hall closet to pull out a game box, one you've never seen. Oh, the mental torment, having to learn all those rules. It just happened to me a couple of months ago at my son's home in Southern California. I'm not a game guy, but I agreed to play for the sake of family "fun."

So, someone has to explain the rules (that would be the truth), and you listen. You ask this person to repeat what he or she has just said, while others re-explain what somebody else just explained. You think deeply until your brain hurts, but nothing seems to make sense. So you beg them to play the game some other night, to let you take the rules home with you, so you can study them carefully or even memorize a few of them. That way you can play the game when you feel more prepared.

Yet your friends won't let you go: "Let's just play!" they insist. "That's the only way you're going to learn, and we're sure you'll like it!"

"OK," you respond sheepishly, knowing that the next hour will probably be painful and humiliating.

What happens next? A test, a crisis, but it's the only way you'll learn the rules. You do something wrong. You break one of the rules. Laughing at you and lunging at your game piece, your friends shout, "No! You can't do that!"

"I didn't know that," you protest.

"Well, you do now," your friends exclaim.

And there goes your little green chip, back twelve spaces.

Off the Subject?

Oh, that's right. I'm supposed be writing a book about worship. OK, then, how about this Bible verse: "Therefore, if you are offering your gift at the altar and there remember that your brother has something against you, leave your gift there in front of the altar. First go and be reconciled to your brother; then come and offer your gift" (Mt 5:23-24). Leave your gift? Stop right in the middle of a song and walk out of church? Who's ever done that? Frankly, it's a command in the Bible I've never seen obeyed in any church in any setting anywhere.

Can you imagine? Someone actually getting up and walking

out of the house of God because he or she is so convicted of unforgiveness? Or because that person realizes he or she hasn't done everything he or she can to heal a relationship? Oh, sure, people get up and walk out of church for all kinds of other reasons, but not because the Word of God is touching them so deeply!

Worship is *not* a private affair, and if I understand Jesus correctly here in Matthew 5:23, God doesn't want our religion unless it *transforms* our relationships with others. This sounds a lot like the Great Commandment: "'Love the Lord your God with all your heart and with all your soul and with all your strength and with all your mind; *and*, 'Love your neighbor as yourself'"" (Lk 10:27). I heard someone say one time that the true test of our faith is if we love one another as much as we love Jesus. That's just a more radical way to say, "If anyone says, 'I love God,' yet hates his brother, he is a liar. For anyone who does not love his brother, whom he has seen, cannot love God, whom he has not seen" (1 Jn 4:20).

Worshiping God and relating in a godly way to his people are mutually inclusive. Worship is in vain and useless if you make no attempt to reconcile broken relationships, and conversely, if you don't worship, if you don't spend time in God's presence, you likely won't be troubled by the fact that your brother has something against you. Worship happens when we turn our hearts toward God, but God's presence in worship turns our hearts toward others. It's all part of the transformational power of worship. The title of Warren Weirsbe's book on worship says it all: *Real Worship: It Will Change Your Life.*

The Transformation Triangle

Let me pull all this good teaching into a visual. Imagine a triangle. You can make one by touching your thumbs and forefingers together. Try it. Now imagine this: the word TRUTH is at the top of the triangle. That's where transformation begins. Hold up you hands and make that triangle again. Now open your index fingers. In comes the truth of God's Word, revealing what needs to be changed, as Paul wrote that "through the law we become conscious of sin" (Rom 3:20). Next, at the bottom two corners of the triangle (on those little flaps of skin between your thumbs and forefingers) think of the words CRISIS and FRIENDSHIP.

Transformation, then, is the result of these three things:

- **truth**, that is, biblical principles (the rules of the game).
- a **test** of the truth in real-life experiences (playing the game): "Consider it pure joy, my brothers, whenever you face trials of many kinds, because you know that the testing of your faith develops perseverance. Perseverance must finish its work so that you may be mature" (Jas 1:2-4).
- significant **friendships** (people helping you learn the game): "Therefore confess your sins to each other and pray for each other so that you may be healed" (Jas 5:16).

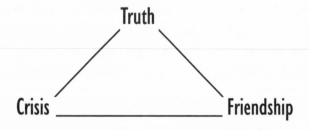

The Transformational Power of the Holy Spirit

Truth + crisis + friendships = transformation is a clever formula, but it is missing the power factor: *the special presence of God.* In the last chapter, when we talked about the special presence of God, I left out something terribly important there, too. I didn't really tell you the most significant thing we can know about the special presence of God. The *shekinah,* you see, is not just a vaporous, swirling cloud of divine energy, sort of like that violent, thunderous mess at the very end of the motion picture *Raiders of the Lost Ark.* No, very simply,

> *The shekinah, the glory of God, the anointing, that wonder-working, special presence of Jahweh was and is a Person: **the Holy Spirit.***[3]

Back to the transformational triangle: TRUTH at the top, CRISIS and FRIENDSHIP at the bottom corners, and now in the center of it all, the power of the Holy Spirit. He alone is the Agent of change and the Power who transforms us. He, the Spirit of God, inspired the Bible and makes its *truth* come alive in our hearts. He, the Spirit of God, guides and comforts us in every *crisis.* And he, the Spirit of God, ministers to us through family and *friendships.* Here's the graphic one more time:

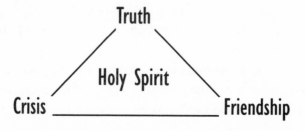

Furthermore, if worship is a gateway into the *shekinah,* into the special presence of God, then worship is an encounter with the transforming power of the Holy Spirit. John Chisum, who is on the staff of Integrity Music, writes that "without a genuine encounter with God, true worship hasn't occurred."

Contemporary Worship?

Honestly, I've always been a bit troubled by the term "contemporary worship," which has been pioneered almost entirely by "charismatic" or "full gospel" churches, congregations that have no hang-ups with such manifestations of the Spirit as speaking in tongues, healing, prophetic utterances, and other miracles. Virtually all of the "contemporary choruses," sung now in every imaginable church and denomination, were written by "Spirit-filled" people. In fact, the ten-year anniversary issue of *Charisma* magazine identified worship as the principal contribution of the "charismatic movement."

Out of these Spirit-born choruses has come "contemporary worship." (Here goes another apple cart.) Contemporary worship has tried to capture the life and power of Spirit-filled, Spirit-led worship, and certainly God is blessed any time his people worship him in any way they can. Yet contemporary worship, where style is often more important than substance, is a stepchild of true worship. Contemporary worship is about singing the right songs in the right way. True worship, on the other hand, is meant to be an encounter with the transforming presence of God, so those who lead true worship, as important as music may be to any of them, want nothing more than to lead people right into the presence of God.

Sally Morganthaler subtitles her best-selling book on worship *Inviting Unbelievers into the Presence of God.* Capturing some of what I've been saying in this chapter, she writes, "A true encounter with God leaves us with a lot more than good feelings. It leaves us with changed hearts and calls us to changed lives. Very simply, to experience God's presence is to be transformed from the inside out.... Where is this transformation today? More and more of us are leaving worship centers and sanctuaries without even so much as a mar on our glossy finish."[4]

"No one who has experienced the incomprehensible, ineffable presence of almighty God has escaped unchanged, untouched, unconfronted," writes John Chisum. "If our present-day worship does not result in a personal encounter with the holiness of God, it does not qualify as true worship."[5]

Transformed From Glory to Glory

Perhaps no other single passage of the Bible is clearer on the transforming power of the Holy Spirit than 2 Corinthians 3. Introducing us to the theme of the glory of God by retelling how Moses, after his visit with God on Sinai, had to cover his shimmering face, the apostle Paul contrasts Moses' "fading glory" with the changeless and life-changing glory of the work of the Spirit.

Paul even implies that reading and studying the Word of God is a lifeless pursuit without the illuminating work and transforming power of the Holy Spirit: "For to this day the same veil remains when the old covenant is read.... Even to this day when Moses [the Pentateuch] is read, a veil covers their hearts" (2 Cor 3:14-15). In other words, we need more than raw truth; we need an encounter with God's special presence:

Now the Lord is the Spirit, and where the Spirit of the Lord is, there is freedom. And we, who with unveiled faces all reflect the Lord's glory, are being transformed into his likeness with ever-increasing glory, which comes from the Lord, who is the Spirit.

2 CORINTHIANS 3:17-18

It's crystal-clear. The Holy Spirit is the Agent of miraculous transformation in the lives of God's people, and to worship, to touch the glory, to experience the *shekinah,* to encounter the Spirit is to be changed deeply and forever. Furthermore, you and I, as "temples of the Holy Spirit," have within us the capacity to offer the power of transformation to the people God brings into our lives, as Paul adds in 2 Corinthians 4:6-7, "For God, who said, 'Let light shine out of darkness,' made his light shine in our hearts to give us the light of the knowledge of *the glory of God* [the *shekinah*] in the face of Christ [in contrast to the face of Moses]. But we have this treasure [the glory, the Spirit] in jars of clay to show that this all-surpassing [and transformational] power is from God and not from us" (2 Cor 4:6-7).

Maybe change is a four-letter word after all: Holy.

And also one with five letters: Spirit.

SIX

PERFECT JESUS, TAKE MY HAND

Since we have a great priest over the house of God, let us draw near to God with a sincere heart in full assurance of faith.
HEBREWS 10:21-22

Ever had to memorize something? Like the Gettysburg Address, or a page from Shakespeare? How about all fifty United States in alphabetical order, or something else just as ridiculous?

How about the Bible? Have you ever memorized a Scripture verse? A whole chapter?

Glance down through the first couple of pages of this chapter. I've listed seven verses from the Psalms. In front of each one is a little box. Take a moment right now and memorize these Scriptures, checking them off as you master them. A magical memory aid is in the endnote.[1]

☐ **Praise the Lord. Praise the Lord,** O my soul (Ps 146:1).
☐ The Lord reigns forever, your God, O Zion, for all generations. **Praise the Lord** (Ps 146:10).
☐ **Praise the Lord.** How good it is to sing praises to our God, how pleasant and fitting to praise him! (Ps 147:1).
☐ **Praise the Lord. Praise the Lord** from the heavens, praise him in the heights above (Ps 148:1).
☐ **Praise the Lord.** Sing to the Lord a new song, his praise in the assembly of the saints (Ps 149:1).

☐ **Praise the Lord.** Praise God in his sanctuary; praise in his mighty heavens (Ps 150:1).

☐ Let everything that has breath **praise the Lord. Praise the Lord** (Ps 150:6).

OK, did you do it? Did you memorize all those verses? If you didn't read the footnote, then you didn't follow the directions carefully. I expected you to memorize only the words in bold: **Praise the Lord**. Occurring over fifty times, "praise the Lord" is, perhaps, the most commonly used phrase in the Psalms, while the English word "praise" is used by itself over two hundred times.[2] There's no better place than the Psalms to learn about praise, and the first thing to learn is that praise is mandatory! It's a command: *Praise the Lord!*

Praising the Lord Over and Over ...

The Psalms *don't*, however, tell us to say "praise the Lord" over and over and over, and my next few paragraphs are going to make some of you feel terribly frustrated. To say "Praise the Lord" is utterly meaningless, unless, of course, you're following the lead of the psalmist and encouraging others to praise the Lord.

Let me put this another way. The Psalms command us to praise the Lord, but nowhere do the Psalms even remotely imply that the way we are to praise the Lord is by saying, "Praise the Lord!" Look at the grammar: "Praise the Lord" is not an expression of worship, it's a command.

What if I tell you that God just healed me miraculously of a dreadful disease? Or that my child, lost for two days, was found safe? Would you say, "Praise the Lord!"? Why is "praise the Lord" such an uncontrollable response when we hear really good news? Think about it: If I share something wonderful God has done in my life, *I'm the one who's praising the Lord.* When your comeback at the end of my story is, "Praise the Lord," you're commanding me to do what I have already done. You see, when I tell you about how good God is in my life, *that is praise.* I just finish giving God glory and praise, and you tell me, "Praise the Lord"? Maybe I should be insulted!

Or, what if you said to me, "Praise the Lord," and suddenly I dropped to my knees, lifted my hands into the air, closed my eyes, and started telling God how grateful I was for some miracle in my life? What would you do? Would you be stunned? You shouldn't be, because I would only be doing what you told me to do when you said, "Praise the Lord."

I know, I'm beating this one into the ground, but here's another way to think of it. Imagine me coming home after a long day. The wonderful aroma of roast beef engulfs me as I open the door. The table is set. The lights are low. Candles are burning. "Wow," I think to myself, "Marilyn has been very thoughtful today," but I say nothing. I don't even look at her, and I don't specifically acknowledge anything she's done. I just blurt out, "Praise the wife! Praise the wife! Praise the wife!" Yep, you'd say I was nuts, and Marilyn, if she didn't think I was just trying to be silly, might suggest that I go out and buy myself some fast food.

OK, what to do? How about saying "alleluia" over and over? Nope, that won't work, either, because "alleluia" is just a Hebrew word that means, literally, "praise the Lord." No, I'm not suggesting that it's some kind of sin if you shout "Alleluia!" or say "Praise the Lord." I've talked about this particular "Christianese" problem off and on for years, and yet I still say, "Praise the Lord," as superficially as anybody else. God have mercy! Yet the deeper lesson here is deeply troubling. Using "praise the Lord" inadvertently, as a kind of Christian conversation filler phrase, betrays how casual and unskilled our worship has become. For so many of God's people, *worship isn't an art, it's a jingle.*

So, where do we go from here? Right back to the Psalms, which not only compel us to praise the Lord but also show us how to praise and worship. Notice in the following Psalm how the writer doesn't just say, "Praise the Lord." Instead, he commands himself to praise the Lord, and then he does it!

> *Praise the Lord, O my soul. [That's the command to myself, so now do it...] O Lord my God, you are very great; you are clothed with splendor and majesty. He wraps himself in light as with a garment; he stretches out the heavens like a tent.*
>
> PSALM 104:1-2

How to Worship: With a Pure Heart

What else can we learn from the Psalms about true worship? First, start with a pure heart. I know, this sounds really basic, because we all understand that worship is inside out. Even the most uninformed person would be quick to say that God looks at the heart, and what our lives look like on the outside matters nothing if we have sick souls. The Bible has a nasty word for that kind of disconnect between heart and life: *hypocrisy,* which is derived from an ancient Greek theater term meaning "to put on the mask." Technically, an actor is a "hypocrite."

In 1 Corinthians 13, Paul contrasts love, the core value of the

Christian life, with five things so many of us believe are really important to God:

- spiritual gifts ("tongues of men and of angels")
- knowledge ("can fathom all mysteries")
- mega-faith ("faith that can move mountains")
- self-sacrifice ("give all I possess")
- passion ("surrender my body to the flames")

Nothing, no, nothing is comparable to love, and all of these potentially loveless things are like an annoying "gong" or a "clanging symbol," like the alarm clock you set, by mistake, to go off at three in the morning. Gifts, knowledge, faith, self-sacrifice, passion—they are "nothing," and "nothing" is to be gained from them without a heart of love. Good behavior, even good "spiritual" practices are worthless without a pure heart, a "fixed heart."[3]

Here's how the psalmist addresses this matter:

Who may ascend the hill of the Lord? Who may stand in his holy place? He who has clean hands and a pure heart, who does not lift up his soul to an idol or swear by what is false. He will receive blessing from the Lord and vindication from God his Savior.

PSALM 24:3-5

"The hill of the Lord" is Zion, and "the holy place" is the spot on which the ark rested. If this is a song of David, it's a reference to his tabernacle, a breezy, veil-less tent pitched on the high place of Jerusalem where the temple of Solomon would one day take its place. So who can go there? Who can access the special presence of God? Who can enjoy the radiant *shekinah*? The answer: a person who lives right, one who doesn't have a "mixed" heart, somebody who loves God and not a lot of other things, too. Oh, and you can trust what this person says. His or her word is as good as gold.

Pure Heart or Perfect Heart?

So it's the righteous ones who can enter freely into the holy place and experience the presence of God. But wait a minute. Am I suggesting that getting into the presence of God is based on what we do, on our righteousness? Yes and no, and I think it's really important to clarify this. In fact, this may be one of the most important things I say in this book, certainly in this chapter, on how to worship.

You see, anytime we talk about God and how to know and experience him, nearly everyone feels at least a tinge of uncertainty, a flash of fear. I can hear you now: "How can I touch God? I'm not worthy. And now you just showed me Psalm 24, and that's not me. I only dream of becoming the person David is describing in this psalm. I guess I'll never ascend the hill of God and appropriate his promises."

Let me explain this and help you find freedom in your daily relationship with God and in those times you give yourself to worship: *There's a difference between a pure heart and a perfect heart.* First, before anything can happen between you and the holy, unapproachable God, a pure heart isn't good enough. You have to have a *perfect heart.* Your heart must be sinless and guileless, a heart with all the right motives, twenty-four/seven.

Now you're probably really feeling badly! "That's not possible!"

you protest. Oh yes it is! It's the gospel. Check this out: "I am not ashamed of the gospel," Paul wrote,

> *because it is the power of God for the salvation of everyone who believes: first for the Jew, then for the Gentile. For in the gospel a righteousness from God is revealed, a righteousness that is by faith from first to last, just as it is written: "The righteous will live by faith."*
>
> ROMANS 1:16-17

The gospel, that is, the Good News, is "righteousness from God," which means *being perfectly righteous does not depend on us, but on God in us.*

It's the Gospel Truth!

Some people like to say that all religions are essentially the same, and in the end, they all lead to the same God. This could not be further from the truth, even though there is some truth in the statement. There are common elements, like the Golden Rule, in every religion. This statement is also true in the sense that all the religions of the world are essentially the same *except the Christian faith.*

Followers of Jesus are not just unique among the followers of, let's say, Buddha or Mohammed, with clever ideas all their own. No, Christianity isn't just one more holy horse of a different color. It's another species. If all the religions of the world are fish, for example, then Christianity is a whale. We're all swimming in the same ocean, but fish are fish and whales are not.

How can I be so bold, so "intolerant"? The explanation is

right there in Romans: "In the gospel a righteousness from God is revealed." This is radical, extraordinary grace, and no other world religion is even in the same universe, because the core of every other religious system is human effort, righteousness *from us*, instead of "righteousness *from God*." All the *other* religions of the world are essentially the same, because all of them, without exception, teach that somehow we have to figure out a way to get to God.

In blazing contrast, Christianity is about God figuring out how to get to us—and sending his Son into a godless, rebellious world, because none of us really want his help, at least not on his terms. Grace, in the New Testament, is not God's divine assistance for those who are giving it their very best. Instead, it's his radical, self-initiated intervention in the lives of those who have no hope. The gospel is the Good News of salvation. "Religion" is the bad news of "slavation."

"To the man who does not work but trusts God who justifies the wicked, his faith is credited as righteousness" (Rom 4:5). God justifies the *wicked*?! Say what? How can God do that? Because all have sinned, and fall everyone short of his glory. God doesn't help those who help themselves, he *"justifies the wicked."* What grace!

Abraham, Paul's perfect example of righteousness by faith, is as good a man as you'll ever find. Abraham, who is claimed as the father of each of the three great monotheistic religions: Judaism, Christianity, and Islam. Yes, Abraham, the man who could not be righteous enough to save his own soul, who, because he feared for his own life, gave his wife to a pagan king and told the man Sarah was his sister (see Gn 20:1-2)!

> *What then shall we say that Abraham, our forefather, dis-*
> *covered in this matter [of righteousness by faith]? If, in fact,*
> *Abraham was justified by works, he had something to boast*
> *about—but not before God. What does the Scripture say?*
> *"Abraham believed God, and it was credited to him as*
> *righteousness."*
>
> ROMANS 4:1-3

It's the gospel truth: righteous *from God*. It's "amazing grace."
How sweet it is. Grace made a wicked man like me perfect
before God. Yes, you can have a perfect heart! When you are
born again, you receive a new nature, you are regenerated, re-
GENE-erated. You get new DNA, the flawless DNA of the Son
of God. You don't have to clean your garments; you trade them
in for the robes of Christ's righteousness (see Zec 3:1-4). When
you become a Christian, all things become new, inside and out.
Maybe you don't *feel* perfect, but from God's point of view you
are perfect, because now when God sees you, he sees his Son in
you and on you.

Nothing More to Do

When Jesus died on the cross, his last words were, "It is finished,"
an extraordinary expression in the original Greek that means
"absolutely and totally done." Or even "paid in full." It's like Jesus
was announcing, "What I've done with my life and now my death
here on the cross has been utterly perfect," for which the Bible can
make another outrageous claim: "By one sacrifice [Jesus] has made
perfect forever those who are being made holy" (Heb 10:14).
Notice the two basic components of salvation in this verse:

1. In Christ, you and I have been made perfect *forever*. It's the *perfect heart* we'd do anything for but can't ever seem to do enough to get. The good news is that a perfect heart is ours for the asking, by faith, an opportunity for a once-and-forever event the Bible calls "justification."

2. Once you get that perfect heart, though, the journey isn't over, because the new nature inside of you has to take over. Specifically, the new nature has to rule the old you. "Therefore," Paul writes, "do not let sin reign in your mortal body so that you obey its evil desires" (Rom 6:12). The Bible call this process of change "sanctification," that is, "being made holy." Over time, it's what makes our hearts purer and purer.

Off the Subject Again ...

Can you hear the screeching tires? I'm coming to a quick stop down a side road so we can get back to the main road of the book: worship. Here's the lesson: worship is not about us doing as well as we can. Worship is about God doing everything *perfectly!* Worship is not so much about us coming to God as it is about God making himself known and available to us. From start to finish, worship is and must be grace-based.

What's the meaning, then, of Psalm 24? Remember, we were there a few pages ago: "Who may ascend the hill of the Lord? He who has ... a pure heart." Here's what I take this to mean: We have free access to God, *anytime, anywhere,* because of the perfect, finished work of Christ.

*Since we have a great priest over the house of God, let us draw
near to God with a sincere heart in full assurance of faith,
having our hearts sprinkled to cleanse us from a guilty conscience and having our bodies washed with pure water.*
HEBREWS 10:21-22

God the Father is close at hand whenever we need him, but the
Bible is also really clear that the things we do can release *or* hinder and limit the work of God in us. For example, let's look at
how we treat others: "Husbands, in the same way be consider-
ate as you live with your wives, and treat them with respect as
the weaker partner and as heirs with you of the gracious gift of
life, so that nothing will hinder your prayers" (1 Pt 3:7).

We even have the potential to offend the Holy Spirit: "Do
not grieve the Holy Spirit of God, with whom you were sealed
for the day of redemption" (Eph 4:30). What are some of the
ways we might grieve the Spirit? Paul continues, "Get rid of all
bitterness, rage and anger, brawling and slander, along with
every form of malice. Be kind and compassionate to one another,
forgiving each other, just as in Christ God forgave you" (Eph
4:31-32).

There they are again, the two sides of salvation: (1) you're
sealed until the day of redemption (justification), and (2) don't
grieve the Holy Spirit of God (sanctification). In worship terms,
if the *special* presence of God and the *glory* of God and the *shekinah* are synonymous with the Holy Spirit, then to grieve the
Spirit is to risk missing out on the powerful blessing of God's
special presence for every little thing in your daily life.

When God created the heavens and the earth and all that's in
them, he wove into the fabric of creation the laws of sowing and
reaping, blessing and judgment, reward and reprisal. "Give and

it will be given to you" is an example of the law of reward. Jump off a building, and the law of reprisal kicks in. Or just try ignoring God's moral laws, like what the Bible says about adultery and fornication. People don't get sexually transmitted diseases just because God is irritated with their behavior. No, judgment is in the system. It's truth or consequences.

How to Worship: With *Your* Heart

OK, so I'm saved by grace, through faith, and as Martin Luther declared, "Here I stand." The act and art of worship, though, releases the blessings of my salvation as I enter the Holy Place of God and experience his special presence, the Holy Spirit. This is why I need *both* a perfect heart and a pure heart.

Yet before we get to "full body praise" in the next chapter, there's one more thing about which you need to feel comfortable. You need to know that worship not only begins in the heart and in a pure heart; it also has to start with *your* heart, that is, what makes you uniquely you. Never forget that the Holy Spirit working through you fits the shape that God made you. Not that the experience of worship will always feel comfortable, but God won't force you into some expressive praise that will leave you needing physical therapy!

You are who God made you, you have a set of life experiences uniquely your own, and who you are is all God has to work with! He will never be as impatient with you as some of your family and friends! "Do not conform any longer to the pattern of this world" (Rom 12:2), Paul wrote. Or, as I've heard this translated, "Don't let the world press you into its mold." Don't let other people squeeze you into theirs, either!

I'm a pretty loud person. It's amazing to me that I get paid for giving my opinion, and people actually like it when I do it passionately! I know, that's not a deeply spiritual definition of preaching, but by now you should have discovered that I have an offbeat way of looking at things.

My dear wife, on the other hand, is quiet, refined, and demure. In thirty years of church ministry, I can't remember a single instance when Marilyn has offended someone. She'd be the first to admit she's not perfect, but in that lovely, gentle part of her, she's as perfect as it gets.

We are so different! For me, expressive worship has come a bit more naturally than for my wife, although, having been raised a conservative Lutheran from an ethnic German family, jumping up and down for God is something I had to learn at the World Series, not in church. But I've come a long way! So has Marilyn, but "a long way" for her is still fairly reserved.

How about you? What's the shape of your clay pot? How has God made you inside? What unique ethnic and cultural experiences have painted the picture of your life?

John Denver in Trinidad and Tobago

Just before we get on to the next chapter, which is about the practice of worship, let me tell you an amazing story about worship "style" and the silliness of trying to squeeze others into our mold. For years I spoke annually in an incredible spiritual life conference in the remote Carribean island nation of Trinidad and Tobago. The country has two major islands, hence the double name, and Tobago sounds like bagel, not toboggan.

Anyway, there I was, the only white face in the room of over a thousand people singing the praises of God. Well, at least they were singing the praises of God the way their worship leaders had learned at a North American conference for worship leaders. All their songs had that John Denver sound, melodious and gentle.

I looked around, and only a few people were really worshiping God, although the worship leaders seemed somewhere between heaven and earth. That was another problem. With eyes shut tighter than a submarine hatch, they kept singing the same chorus over and over. I think that was something they had learned in North America, too, that in order to really press into God, you have to wring every possible blessing out of every word in every line of the chorus.

After over an hour of "worship," I think we had sung two or three songs. And impatient, type-A me, well, I'm dyin'. And I may be wrong on this, but it seemed to me that most of the people there were not "entering in," either—until something outrageous happened later in the service.

After their corporate singing, they had a Jamaican guest do "special music," not to be confused with "worship." One huge grin and a few bars of reggae later, the place was rockin' for God! The "special music," so culturally relevant, launched an explosion of the most exuberant and joyful time of praise you could ever imagine.

You had to be there.

Although the "special music" lasted only about ten or fifteen minutes, the glory fell, and those people touched the heart of God. The worship fit perfectly their dark clay jars.

Even the only white face in the crowd (me) was really blessed.

Praise the Lord!

Whoops. I'm not supposed to say that.

SEVEN

WHOLEHEARTED, FULL-BODIED PRAISE

Praise the Lord.
How good it is to sing praises to our God,
how pleasant and fitting to praise him!

PSALM 147:1

SILENCE. ENTERING THE HOUSE OF GOD.

That's what the signs warned, the ones placed conspicuously over the two entry portals to the dark, cavernous sanctuary. To make sure everyone saw them, the inscriptions were engraved in large, old-English lettering.

You're guessing wrong. I wasn't in an Anglican cathedral in London. I was in downtown Phoenix, and the huge, plain-Jane, historic building, left vacant by its increasingly suburban congregation, was a temporary facility for our church during a construction project.

Pausing before one of those castle-like doors, I pondered the sign's deeper meaning. "Hmm, SILENCE," I thought. "Of all the things they *could* have said about the house of God, why would they post *that* message over the entrances to the worship center?" Why couldn't it have been something like ...

COME, LET US WORSHIP THE LORD

Or, like the sign over one of the doors into our church,

MY HOUSE SHALL BE A HOUSE OF PRAYER
FOR ALL NATIONS
or even
JESUS IS LORD!

But no, the Word of God for that old, Bible-preaching church was *silence*. Fortunately, someone in our congregation took it upon him- or herself to correct the *silence* part of the signs by covering that word with brown cardboard patches that read:

Rejoice!
ENTERING THE HOUSE OF GOD

I think they got the idea from the Psalms: "I rejoiced with those who said to me, 'Let us go to the house of the Lord'" (Ps 122:1).

The assumption in many places where Christians worship is that "silence" and "reverence" are virtual synonyms, yet, surprisingly, these two words mean very different things in the Bible. I'll come back to the specifics of this a little later in this chapter, but the larger questions are: What does the Bible say about church, how we do church, and how we worship in church? Are we willing to embrace the Bible, and obey it, even if it's culturally uncomfortable?

We've already learned that Scripture, especially the Psalter, commands us to praise the Lord. When the psalmists shout, "Praise the Lord," it's not as though they can't think of anything else to tell God, like so many of us. No, the broken-record mandate of the Psalms, "praise the Lord," comes to us not in the monotones of meaningless repetition or the superficial filler-phrases of Christian-speak. Instead, "praise the Lord" is a real command, repeated throughout the Psalms to remind us of our life purpose: "to glorify God and to enjoy him forever."

How to Praise the Lord

Funny, though, how readily people can say "praise the Lord" without a second thought about *how* they're supposed to do it, even though the Psalms are just as clear about the *practice* of worship—*how* to praise God—as they are about insisting we do it. Worship, the Psalms teach, involves things like being noisy and not silent. Using drums, or dancing, or raising our hands. Singing, of course. Even shouting and feeling emotion. Yet somehow this is where everything seems to break down, because *how* to praise the Lord, even though the Bible is quite clear on this, is surprisingly controversial.

Why is there so much resistance to expressive worship as taught in the Bible? I have several thoughts. *First, open and expressive worship is not part of our culture.* Did you know that at the turn of the twentieth century, global Christianity was 90 percent white? And that by the year 2000, Christianity had become 90 percent nonwhite? For most of the population of the world, knowing God is not primarily mental, and worship is an expressive, even sensual experience, which leads me to my *second* point.[1]

In our cultural isolation, many of us North American Christians have made little or no attempt to understand other cultures, or even the culture in which the Bible was written. Did you know, for example, that worship around the ancient tabernacle of Moses, where the Israelites first experienced the *shekinah,* excited all five senses? Try, if you can, to imagine the sights and sounds of the music; the colorful pageantry and symbolism; the "drink offering" and the savory roasted lamb of the Passover meal; the aroma of the incense, "a sweet fragrance unto the Lord." Worship in the Old Testament was both transcendent and earthy, wholehearted and full-bodied.[2]

Top Ten Reasons Why Church People Can't Get Into Worship[3]

10. It's too cold in here.
9. The music is too loud.
8. I can't hear the singers.
7. We should sing more hymns.
6. I don't like singing hymns.
5. I don't know these songs.
4. I have too much on my mind.
3. I just can't sing very well.
2. It's getting really hot in here.

And the number one reason why church people can't get into worship:

1. I JUST DON'T FEEL LIKE IT!

Holy Noise

Third, deeply rooted in these cultural issues, is the idea introduced at the beginning of this chapter: *reverence somehow has come to mean silence, while public enthusiasm for God is often scorned as "emotionalism."* Yet listen to what the Bible teaches so clearly about enthusiastic people in the presence of the living God:

After this I looked and there before me was a great multitude that no one could count, from every nation, tribe, people and language, standing before the throne and in front of the Lamb.... And they cried out in a loud voice: "Salvation belongs to our God, who sits on the throne, and to the Lamb." Then a voice came from the throne, saying: "Praise our God, all you his servants, you who fear him, both small and great!" Then I heard what sounded like a great multitude, like the roar of rushing waters and like loud peals of thunder, shouting: "Hallelujah! For our Lord God Almighty reigns."

REVELATION 7:9-10;19:5-6

To me, this doesn't sound very silent! For people who are uncomfortable with loud, expressive worship, heaven may seem like a strange place. In fact, in Revelation, a book of the Bible that features heaven prominently, silence happens only once and then for only about thirty minutes.[4] And it's not a good thing:

When he opened the seventh seal, there was silence in heaven for about half an hour. And I saw the seven angels who stand before God, and to them were given seven trumpets.... The first angel sounded his trumpet, and there came hail and fire mixed with blood, and it was hurled down upon the earth. A third of the earth was burned up, a third of the trees were burned up, and all the green grass was burned up.

REVELATION 8:1-2, 7

The sign in the old church read, "Silence. Entering the House of God." A sign here in Revelation 8 might read: "Silence. The Judgment of God Is About to Begin." Frankly, I think both signs communicate essentially the same thing: fear.

Certainly, as a personal spiritual discipline, silence is laudable, even necessary. At this very moment, I'm writing this book at a lovely retreat center, Community of Living Water, in the verdant Verde River Valley in central Arizona. (Not every square inch of our state is sand and rock!) The ministry here hosts weekend camps, but during the week, people come for personal prayer retreats, so they have signs everywhere encouraging silence. Talky man that I am, someone on their staff had to remind me kindly that, though I may be here to work, others are here to seek God in a one- or two-day non-talking, silent season of solitude.

Unholy Silence

Silence can also be a godly thing for husbands and wives: "Everyone should be quick to listen, slow to speak and slow to become angry" (Jas 1:19). Silence is good! But not necessarily in worship. Doing a Bible word search a few years ago, I discovered to my complete surprise that silence is hardly used once in the Psalms or anywhere else in the Bible as a component of worship. In fact, over and over, the Bible uses the term "silence" negatively. The following verses from the Psalms are typical:

- When I kept *silent*, my bones wasted away through my groaning all day long (Ps 32:3).
- But when I was *silent* and still, not even saying anything good, my anguish increased (Ps 39:2).
- Unless the Lord had given me help, I would soon have dwelt in *the silence of death* (Ps 94:17).

- It is not the dead who praise the Lord, *those who go down to silence* (Ps 115:17).
- You turned my wailing into dancing; you removed my sackcloth and clothed me with joy, that my heart may sing to you *and not be silent*. O Lord my God, I will give you thanks forever (Ps 30:11-12).

Irreverent Silence

Have I made my point? In the Bible, silence is nearly always a negative thing. Silence is not a synonym for reverence. In fact, there are times when silence may be irreverent! That's what happened on Palm Sunday, a day in the life of Jesus when noise was holy, silence was unholy:

> *When [Jesus] came near the place where the road goes down the Mount of Olives, the whole crowd of disciples began joyfully to praise God in loud voices for all the miracles they had seen: "Blessed is the king who comes in the name of the Lord! Peace in heaven and glory in the highest!" Some of the Pharisees in the crowd said to Jesus, "Teacher, rebuke your disciples!" [Tell them to stop the irreverent, blathering noise!] "I tell you," he replied, "if they keep quiet, the stones will cry out."*
>
> LUKE 19:37-40

There you have it, irreverent silence!

Yes, loud noise can be painful! As a former radical sixties hippie friend of mine, Sean Donaldson, said to me recently, "I never thought I'd see the day when I'd be telling *my* kids,

"Turndownthatmusic!"

Yet, noise isn't inherently wrong. Sheer sound has a power of its own, for good or for evil, like the mesmerizing dissonance of a rock concert. Or the boom of July Fourth fireworks above a military band concert on the steps of the Jefferson Memorial in Washington, D.C. Or a Christian concert (some people think that's an oxymoron, like reverent noise). Fans roaring for their favorite team is called a "home field *advantage*"!

I've already taken you out to the ball game, the 2001 World Series, in chapter one. At most sporting events I've attended, including football and basketball, the management has to remind fans to yell and scream. Up on the scoreboard, in brazen electric lights, flashes the giant word *NOISE* (kind of like those big *SILENCE* signs in that old church, only just the opposite). That never happened at the World Series game I attended, though, as the energy sustained itself through all nine innings, breaking into eardrum-shattering pandemonium every time "we" scored a run.

Sound Advice

But noise like this in church? We've been told that if your ears hurt in church something must be wrong! Well, not that your ears should hurt in church. Maybe the sound system really does need fixing, or the sound guy needs firing! Just as silence is not a synonym for reverence, noise is not just another word for worship. Yet if noise *never* happens in church, that's a problem, too!

Many Psalms say things like this, "Clap your hands, all you nations; shout to God with cries of joy. How awesome is the

Lord Most High, the great King over all the earth! He subdued nations under us, peoples under our feet" (Ps 47:1-3). So when and where is this supposed to happen? When we all die and go to heaven? That's not even slightly implied here. The time to shout to God with "ear-splitting sound" (that's the meaning of the Hebrew word "shout") is right now. Probably in and around the house of the Lord:

> *With praise and thanksgiving they sang to the Lord: "He is good; his love to Israel endures forever." And all the people gave a great shout of praise to the Lord, because the foundation of the house of the Lord was laid. But many of the older priests and Levites and family heads, who had seen the former temple, wept aloud when they saw the foundation of this temple being laid, while many others shouted for joy. No one could distinguish the sound of the shouts of joy from the sound of weeping, because the people made so much noise. And the sound was heard far away.*
>
> Ezra 3:11-13

Not all the worship in the Bible is just a bunch of noise. The Psalms, you see, not only tell us to praise the Lord and to make holy noise, they also command us to sing and use musical instruments, and centuries later the apostle Paul added this important guideline for public worship: "God is not a God of disorder, but of peace.... [Therefore] everything should be done in a fitting and orderly way" (1 Cor 14:33, 40). In other words, noise for noise's sake is not worship.

Instruments of God

Noisy (hopefully well-played) instruments, though, are acceptable! Psalm 150 is a smorgasbord of sound and rhythm: *Praise the Lord.* There it is again, that now infamous three-word command, followed by multiple suggestions on where, when, and how you should praise him. Where's a good place to worship? *Praise God in his sanctuary; praise him in his mighty heavens.* That would be in church and in a park on a starry night.

For what should we be praising him? In case you can't think of a reason, the Psalms are a good source of inspiration for that, too: *Praise him for his acts of power; praise him for his surpassing greatness.*

And just how should we go about praising him? Psalmist of God, tell us something about the arts of worship: *Praise him with the sounding of the trumpet, praise him with the harp and lyre, praise him with tambourine and dancing.* Yes, dancing! Both rehearsed and spontaneous. *Praise him with the strings and flute, praise him with the clash of cymbals, praise him with resounding cymbals.*

A guy in our church took that last statement literally, the one about the "resounding cymbals." Not every week, but often enough, he brought his very own blue-velvet-cased cymbals right into that old sanctuary where we were supposed to be silent. Seldom noticed by those around him and *never* noticed by those in front of him, he'd slide those golden disks out of their shimmery bag, and just when folks were really getting excited about God in praise, he'd hold them high above his head and ... WHAM!!! People in the row in front of him always thought it was the end of the world. I can still see them bowing their heads, not in prayer, but in self-defense!

So make loud and joyous music to the God of music! "Sing to the Lord a new song; sing to the Lord, all the earth. Sing to the Lord, praise his name; proclaim his salvation day after day" (Ps 96:1-2). *Let everything that has breath praise the Lord. Praise the Lord!* (Ps 150:6).

Whole-Hearted, Full-Bodied Praise

Years ago, my dear mother-in-law and I were talking about praise and worship, and how different it was in her traditional church, compared with the more radical, contemporary services in my church. Invariably, in discussions like that, the practice of "lifting our hands to God" always seems to come up. Why would you do that *in church?* To a typical traditionalist, lifting hands in the sanctuary is distracting, even weird. Yet it's in the Bible!

When I showed my mother-in-law a couple of places in Scripture where lifting hands in praise and prayer was normal, she said softly but firmly, "I'll *never* do that." No, she wouldn't, even though in the liturgy for vespers services in the Lutheran Church, she (and I) sang, "Let the lifting up of my hands be as the evening sacrifice."[5] We just never did it. Well, later in life, she did. From time to time she raised her hands in worship, even though she remained a devout Lutheran until the day she went to be with Jesus.

Think about it. Why is it so terribly offensive in some church settings if people raise their hands in worship? At the very least, it makes many people feel self-conscious and embarrassed. Well, for your faith's sake, you should watch just one hour of "Sports Center" on ESPN. Or just the sports highlights on the local evening news.

You will not, *no, not ever,* see a home run, a touchdown, a slam-dunk, a hole-in-one, a winning horse at the Kentucky Derby, a goal at a soccer match between Ireland and France, or a bullfight without fans in the background—*all of them raising their hands to heaven.* I have a thick file of sports highlight photos with both players and masses of people in the grandstands behind them smiling and laughing, *hands in the air.* I guess they're all praising the Lord for letting their team win!

It's a fact: if your kid's little league team wins, or you win the lottery, or just a door prize at the church potluck, you will uncontrollably raise your hands to heaven! It is the most natural way our human bodies express inexpressible joy. Lifting hands is body language for gladness and delight.

Except in church?

Yadah, Yadah, Yadah

The principles and practices of praise and worship are more richly communicated in ancient Hebrew than in just about any other language, perhaps because Hebrew developed in conjunction with the worship of Jahweh. In fact, some Jewish traditions consider Hebrew a miracle language, given directly to Israel by God himself. Unlike our unimaginative, even sterile English vocabulary for worship, the Hebrew language has a rainbow of seven wonderful words, all translated blandly as "praise" in the English Bible.

Each of these Hebrew terms has a unique meaning that gets lost in the translation. For example, two of these seven Hebrew terms for worship, *todah* (Ps 50:23) and *yadah* (Ps 54:6) mean, literally, "to extend the hands to God." You don't have to know Hebrew, though, to decide to lift your hands in praise! In the Bible, people lifted their hands to God for many reasons:

- **As an expression of love:** "O God, you are my God, earnestly I seek you; my soul thirsts for you, my body longs for you, in a dry and weary land where there is no water. I have seen you in the sanctuary and beheld your power and your glory. Because your love is better than life, my lips will glorify you. I will praise you as long as I live, and in your name *I will lift up my hands*" (Ps 63:1-4). "May my prayer be set before you like incense; *may the lifting up of my hands be like the evening sacrifice*" (Ps 141:2).

- **As a sign of vulnerability and surrender to God:** "Ezra opened the book. All the people could see him because he was standing above them; and as he opened it, the people all stood up. Ezra praised the Lord, the great God; and *all the people lifted their hands* and responded, 'Amen! Amen!' Then they bowed down and worshiped the Lord with their faces to the ground" (Neh 8:5-6). "Let us *lift up our hearts and our hands to God* in heaven, and say: 'We have sinned and rebelled and you have not forgiven'" (Lam 3:41-42).

- **As a sign of faith:** "Hear my cry for mercy as I call to you for help, as *I lift up my hands* toward your Most Holy Place" (Ps 28:2). *"I lift up my hands to your commands,* which I love, and I meditate on your decrees" (Ps 119:48).

- **As a symbol of spiritual authority:** "The Amalekites came and attacked the Israelites at Rephidim. Moses said to Joshua, 'Choose some of our men and go out to fight the Amalekites. Tomorrow I will stand on top of the hill with the staff of God in my hands.' So Joshua fought the Amalekites as Moses had ordered, and Moses, Aaron, and Hur went to the top of the hill. *As long as Moses held up his hands,* the Israelites were winning, but whenever he lowered his hands, the Amalekites were winning. When Moses' hands grew tired, they took a stone and put it under him and he sat on it. Aaron and Hur held his hands up—one on one side, one on the other—so that his hands remained steady till sunset" (Ex 17:8-12).

- **As a posture for prayer:** "I want men everywhere to lift up holy hands in prayer..." (1 Tm 2:8).

In Summary ...

To summarize my last couple of chapters, the Bible commands, "Praise the Lord." It also explains how to worship deeply and how to praise expressively:

- With a perfect heart, that is, with faith in the finished work of Christ;
- With a pure heart, that is, with a daily commitment to obey God and live uprightly;
- With your whole heart, that is, with your mind, your will, and your emotions;

- With holy noise;
- With singing and musical instruments;
- With your whole body, with dancing and the arts, with your hands uplifted;
- In truth, according to what God reveals about himself in the Bible; and
- In truth, according to what the Bible says about how to praise and worship.

From Reluctance to Release

Reluctance to do *anything* differently from the way we've always done it is humanly normal, so take heart. You may have an inhibition or two, or a few more questions than I have answers. "Expressive worship" may make you feel uncomfortable. Yet you are reading this book, and you've made it all the way to the end of this chapter! It tells me you must be hungry for more of God in your life, and you are open to experiencing more of his personal presence.

As we wrap up this chapter, let me give you some practical advice: *First, take it one step at time.* Worship is the pursuit of a lifetime and the central activity of eternity. No matter where you are in the practice and experience of worship, there's always much more of God just ahead of you. I've already told you that's the reason we have to live forever in God's presence, because it's going to take an eternity for us to get to know and experience fully our infinite God.

So, there's no urgency. Sometimes God's well-meaning people get themselves in a hurry. Others, in their enthusiasm for God and more meaningful worship, may try to rush you along.

Remember, though, that with God a thousand years is as a day, and a day is as a thousand years. Heaven is not about arriving, it's just the next step in the eternal journey we began when Jesus came into our hearts.

It's bad enough to be frenzied about life, but I'm persuaded that there's nothing worse than being anxious about our relationship with God. Remember, Jesus calmed frantic Martha, "You are worried and upset about many things, but only one thing is needed. Mary has chosen what is better, and it will not be taken away from her" (Lk 10:41-42). To Moses, Jahweh promised, "My Presence will go with you, and I will give you rest," to which Moses responded insightfully, "If your Presence does not go with us, do not send us up from here" (Ex 33:14-15). So wherever you are with God, whatever elements of worship are known or unknown to you, just take the next step. The race of faith is a marathon, not a sprint.

Second, worship the way God made you. Is your family of origin from Africa? Italy? Northern Europe? Latin America? Asia? Are you excitable? Calm? Outgoing? Reserved? Male or female? Born before World War II? In your twenties? From the country? Love the city? *Guess what?!* Every unique thing about you will factor into how you worship.

Third, don't let the way you think God made you or shaped your life in the past become an excuse to stay the same. A few months ago, at a weekend retreat with the governing board of our church, I said something like, "At this point in my life, I'm not going to change." Well, I didn't exactly say that, but that's what people heard, and one of the men on our board gently corrected me for my ill-advised comment.

What I meant to say was, "I know who I am—and who I'm not. At this point in my life, I'm feeling comfortable with who

I am and what God has called me uniquely to do. I can be everything God has made me to be, but I can't be everything everybody expects of me. I can be only who I am in Christ and in his unique purposes for my life." Well, that's a lot different than saying, "I ain't gonna change!" All of us have things to learn, challenges to face, and opportunities to stretch us further into the future and deeper into God.

Fourth, always keep an open heart, especially to what the Bible teaches. Don't make the mistake of making the Bible say whatever makes *you* feel comfortable about God and worship. It's common, now, for people to announce, "I don't believe in *that* kind of God," implying that they've pretty much decided for themselves what their God is going to be like. That, my good readers, is idolatry, coming up with your own sort of god and then bowing down to the deity that's no bigger than your imagination. The designer god in your head isn't God.

Let the Bible be your absolute and final authority on who God is, what he's like, and how to worship and praise him, like the Berean Christians early in the history of the first-century church, who "were of more noble character than the Thessalonians, for they received the message with great eagerness and examined the Scriptures every day to see if what Paul said was true" (Acts 17:11).

Fifth, keep learning about worship. Read books by people who are known for their gift for writing about God and the art of worship. Visit your local Christian bookstore for ideas and resources. Listen to worship leaders from ministries like Hill Song, Integrity, Vineyard, and others. Visit churches where the worship style is different from what you are used to, and if you are white, like me, spend time with Hispanic or African-American or Asian brothers and sisters. Make an effort to make friends cross-culturally and worship with them.

Finally, if you ever have the chance, invest some of your hard-earned money in a short-term mission experience, where you have the opportunity to worship with people in the developing world. It's likely that the more difficult their circumstances, the more deeply you will experience God with them.

EIGHT

MONDAY WORSHIP

Whatever you do, work at it with all your heart,
as working for the Lord, not for men.

COLOSSIANS 3:23

Here a little, there a little.

That's the way I used to write books, until my son's "boss," George Barna, introduced me to what he calls "binge writing," marking out a week on the calendar, getting away from it all, and writing morning, noon, and night. Only certain of us writers are suited for this kind of madness, but it works for me!

So here I am in God's country, cool Cottonwood, Arizona, just two hours north and a few thousand feet higher in elevation than hot Phoenix, where today it's 106 in the shade. As I look over the top of my computer screen, out the sliding-glass door in front of me, I have a magnificent, painting-perfect view of an emerald cottonwood forest hunkering down along ruddy Oak Creek. Yes, there are oaks on Oak Creek, too, but they're upstream a few miles in the world-famous red rocks of Sedona, Arizona.

And there's Jerry out there. The retreat center handyman. Making music to God with what looks like a new red-orange tractor. He's been at it since breakfast. Regrading the parking area. Knocking down weeds in an open field. Back and forth, back and forth. I have my door open, and I can't really decide if his rumbling, whining machine is annoying me. I suppose I'll prefer the silence a little later in the day, maybe after lunch, but *praise the Lord*, Jerry is an absolutely wonderful illustration for this chapter.

Church Without Walls, Worship Without Music

Jerry, you see, is not at church right now. As far as I know, there's no church within several miles, although I know he and his wife attend one not far from here. Furthermore, it's not even "the Lord's Day," it's Wednesday. So he's not dressed for church, either. He's just out there doing his work. Conscientiously. Energetically. He probably isn't even thinking about "spiritual things" right now. As I see him out there, dust clouds swirling behind his tractor, the word "worshiping" doesn't exactly pop into my mind.

Yet whether or not he's singing, or listening to a Christian CD (I can't really tell), *Jerry's work is worship*, and right now he's worshiping God with his whole heart. You've heard the old Disney song "Whistle While You Work"? Well, I thought about titling this chapter "Worship While You Work."

Worship isn't just liturgy, religious singing, or an act of pageantry on a religious day in a religious building. Worship, as we learned in an earlier chapter, is *who you are*. It's the whole of your life, created for God's glory. It's also every little thing you do when you do it for God's sake. Worship, in this sense, is comprehensive. In fact, worship is the consecration of everything in our lives to God: work, family, relationships, possessions, our bodies, sex. When something is sacred, you just think about it differently, use it more reverently.

The Curse of the Spirituality Scale

I know Jerry only a little. I don't know if he's ever taught a Bible study, and I don't think he plays a musical instrument, but right now Jerry's working that tractor as hard as I'm working my computer to write this book, and we're both doing what we're doing to serve God. One of us is not more "spiritual" than the other.

That's a problem, you know. Value judgments. The idea that some people are better than others. Or that what you do is better than what other people do. Or, worst of all, in my view, rating people and what they do on the spirituality scale. Hey, it's common! I mean, wouldn't you just naturally think of me as a spiritual person? After all, I've been in full-time "ministry" for thirty years, and I write books about God. And then there's Jerry. He just drives a tractor and repairs air-conditioning units. He doesn't really do "spiritual" things, or at least that's what we so commonly surmise.

This kind of spirituality-scale thinking is rooted in our unfortunate distinction between secular and sacred, as in, Are you in *the ministry?* Or do you have a *secular* vocation? There's another oxymoron, "secular vocation," because the term "vocation" is derived from the Latin word for "voice," or "call." When the English word "vocation" was first used, it referred to a person's "call," that is, what God created them uniquely to do and become in this life, so that discovering your vocation was much more important than finding a job.[1]

Your work is "spiritual"! Turning your work over *to* God and doing it for God makes your work sacred, yes, just as hallowed as preaching the Bible or going to church. What you do outside of church is no less important to God than what you do inside.

In fact, it could be *more* important! Ministers aren't the only ones who can say, "I'm working for God!"

Moses' Holy Stick

Once upon a time a man named Moses left Egypt to work for his father-in-law, Jethro. Actually, he fled for his life, because he had killed someone, and the Egyptians were looking for him. Before this terrible incident, Moses had had every reason to believe God was setting him up for success. As an infant his life had been miraculously spared, and though a Jew in a pagan land, he grew up in the family of the king. In ancient Egypt, you may know, they called kings "pharaohs."

Well, things didn't work out, and Moses' career took a nose dive from a promising future in the family business of his adoptive father to taking care of goats in some insufferable desert. There he was, mindlessly minding the goats, when God appeared to him in that God-forsaken place. Spoke out of a burning bush. Called him back to Egypt to be the deliverer of the enslaved Jewish people.

"What, you're asking me to be your spokesman? Back there in the court of the Pharaoh?" he queried God. Moses hated his job, but at this point in his life, he couldn't imagine doing anything else, particularly risking his life by returning to Egypt. He was stuck in the wilderness and trapped by his own pain.

"What's that in your hand, Moses?" came the Voice out of the bush. "Why, it's my goat stick. You should know, God. It's a symbol of the hopelessness and drudgery of my life. This stick is my job, it's my lot in life. I'm stuck with this stick, and I hate it."

"Throw it down," said God.

"Gladly," thought Moses. And he did.

SHAZAM! The goat stick became a snake!

The mark of Moses' failure and shame, the most secular thing about him, turned out to be the rod of God! He was holding the miracle-working power of Jahweh right there in his hand and didn't even know it. The past Moses wanted to forget and the present he scorned were about to morph into a tale of biblical proportions. One day he would stretch that same rough stick over the Red Sea, and ...

WHOOSH! The ocean would become a canyon.

Think about it! In a sense, your life and mine—our very future—was in that stick, too! The most "unspiritual," ordinary thing in Moses' life, he found out, was the most "spiritual," extraordinary thing. The goat stick was destined to become the staff of deliverance for millions of Jews.[2]

So what do you have in your hand?

What's your stick?

What is it in your job, your life, that seems so disconnected from God, so meaningless, so painful? Give it another look before you give up. Throw it down. Give it to God. Could it be that God wants to turn your goat stick into a scepter of worship?

Bridging the Gap

Did you know that God's original intention for the Sabbath day was to remind us that everything in our lives is sacred? Every day? Every moment? Every stick? Yes, the Sabbath has its practical benefits as a day of rest from the toilsome labors of the week, a time for the human body to be refreshed and restored. Yet it was meant to be so much more. God gave us the Sabbath as a kind of bridge between our "spiritual" relationship with him and our "practical" relationship with everything else in his creation.

Consider the Ten Commandments. The first three in Exodus 20 spell out how we should relate to God: he's the only One, we must not create our own gods, and we should not take his name in vain. The Fourth Commandment tells us to keep the Sabbath. As God rested from work on the seventh day of Creation, as God looked back on his work and said, "It is good," we, too, should reflect each week on God's provision and care for us.

Shamefully, we look *forward* to the weekend when we don't have to work! T.G.I.F.! Our world is backward and upside down! Instead, we should be shouting, "Thank God it's Monday!" During the first-ever workweek, God didn't look forward to the weekend, saying, "Yeah, it's almost here!" He looked *back* and said, "Yeah, that's good!"

So God gave us the Sabbath to rekindle our love for him and to refocus our thoughts and emotions in order to prepare us for "worship" in every daily moment in the week ahead. The Sabbath (Commandment Four) was designed to interface the "spiritual things" in our relationship with God (Commandments One to Three) with the "practical things" of daily life, namely family, neighbors, and possessions (Commandments Five to Ten).

The holy Seventh Day offers us the opportunity to think of all the other days as holy, too, to make every moment, every activity an act of worship, whether we are going to church on Sunday morning or driving a red-orange tractor on Wednesday afternoon. (There goes Jerry, again. It's now the middle of the afternoon. He's back at it, back and forth.)

Whether or not you're thinking about it, your work is worship, but when you do think about it, it changes everything about how you work. Paul wrote to the Colossians,

Slaves [employees?], obey your earthly masters in everything; and do it, not only when their eye is on you and to win their favor, but with sincerity of heart and reverence for the Lord [sounds like worship]. Whatever you do, work at it with all your heart, as working for the Lord, not for men, since you know that you will receive an inheritance from the Lord as a reward. It is the Lord Christ you are serving.
COLOSSIANS 3:22-24

Worship is not just what you do in church, it's the act of bringing God into everything you do, allowing every moment of your life to honor God. As Paul wrote, "So whether you eat or drink or whatever you do, do it all for the glory of God" (1 Cor 10:31).

Work Is Good

God cursed work when Adam and Eve sinned, but work itself is not a curse. Work happened before sin and the curse: "The Lord God took the man and put him in the Garden of Eden to *work* it and take care of it" (Gn 2:15). He could have been driving a red-orange tractor! And before that, even God worked. So work is a God thing. Work is good, even the most basic forms of work, like gardening in Eden or here in central Arizona.

Many Christians, though, have no sense that their "secular" work is their *ministry*. As a result, their work becomes drudgery, and their job becomes an end in itself. People who don't worship when they work generally work for two reasons: income and identity, which is why our "jobs," in the end, never live up to our expectations. In contrast, the Bible teaches me that *God* is my Provider, not my job, and my identity is who I am in Christ, not where I am in the pecking order. Further-more, according to the Bible, the purpose of work is to worship God and to serve others, and when you work for those reasons, it's like your job is born again.

A few months ago, I was listening to an interview on National Public Radio with an author who was just finishing a book on "religious" universities, like Wheaton, Seattle Pacific, Oral Roberts, or Biola. The author, who did not seem to have a personal religious agenda, had been deeply moved by what she found in her research.

Christian universities offer the full range of studies found at any state university, from medicine to law, art to education, music to public policy, but from a unique perspective, that everything in life, every discipline, every career, every "vocation" relates somehow back to God and his purposes for each of us. This, she discovered, made for graduates who looked at their lives and careers very differently from the way students in secular institutions saw theirs. Those students seemed less certain about their future and seemed to be preparing for careers for very different reasons. Perhaps we could say that, for students at Christian universities, significance is more important than success.

During the course of her research, this author had asked a professor at a Christian college what difference, for example, a God-orientation would make in, let's say, an accounting career. What's religious about accounting? To this the professor replied something like this, "If everyone saw their work as service to God, then perhaps we would not have seen the collapse of Enron."[3]

It's pretty simple. Worship that doesn't work its way out of the church building and into the sanctuary of your personal life just isn't worship. To borrow the words of Paul, worship like that would be nothing more than "a resounding gong or a clanging cymbal." Perhaps this is why church people are sometimes seen as hypocrites.

To love and worship God is to love and respect others, and true worship releases a river of blessing through us to others. So start thinking of your work as a gift from God and use it as a form of worship, that is, as something that brings glory to God.

Go ahead. Worship while you work.

NINE

WARFARE WORSHIP

*May the praise of God be in their mouths and a double-edged
sword in their hands, to inflict vengeance on the nations and
punishment on the peoples, to bind their kings with fetters,
their nobles with shackles of iron, to carry out the sentence
written against them.*

PSALM 149:6-9

Yes, Virginia, there is a devil.

Or, as Paul writes, "Put on the full armor of God so that you
can take your stand against the devil's schemes. For our struggle
is not against flesh and blood, but against the rulers, against the
authorities, against the powers of this dark world and against the
spiritual forces of evil in the heavenly realms" (Eph 6:11-12).

Worship, and who's going to get it, is the central issue of the
universe. Whomever or whatever you worship, directly or indi-
rectly, becomes the highest authority in your life, and wherever
you acknowledge a higher authority, that authority will exercise
control and dominion. Every time you bow down to something, a kingdom is born or built.

Worship is humanity's highest calling, and miraculously, ordinary human worship becomes the throne room and dwelling
place of the Most High God. This means that worship is perhaps the most powerful weapon in the spiritual arsenal of the

believer. Worship enthrones God and dethrones the devil: "The weapons we fight with are not the weapons of the world," wrote Paul. "On the contrary, they have divine power to demolish strongholds" (2 Cor 10:4). Even children are empowered by praise and worship: "From the lips of children and infants you have ordained praise because of your enemies, to silence the foe and the avenger" (Ps 8:2).

Praise and worship exalt our God.

Praise and worship put the devil in his place.

Praise Is Kingdom Activity

Praise is an aggressive affirmation before the audiences of heaven, earth, and hell that Jesus is Lord! Praise is both the confession of your mouth (speaking, singing) that Jesus is Lord and a lifestyle of obedience and service to him. Over against true worship, Satan's ageless obsession has been to depose God and redirect the adoration of the universe to himself. In what is widely believed to be a reference to the downfall of Satan, Isaiah writes,

> *How you have fallen from heaven, O morning star [Lucifer in the King James Version], son of the dawn!... You who once laid low the nations! You said in your heart, "I will ascend to heaven; I will raise my throne above the stars of God; I will sit enthroned on the mount of assembly, on the utmost heights of the sacred mountain.... I will make myself like the Most High."*

ISAIAH 14:12-14

When Jesus came to reestablish God's kingdom on the earth, Satan shrewdly offered him a shortcut to victory, an easy way out of the cross. He proposed to give Jesus authority over all the kingdoms of this world in exchange for a few moments of worship. Satan knew that an instant of praise from the Son of God would have unimaginable consequences.

Whom you praise and what you worship have enormous implications, because whatever you worship will become the master of your soul. Listen to the frightful conditions of the last days: "The whole world was astonished and followed the beast [the Antichrist]. Men worshiped the dragon because he had given authority to the beast, and they also worshiped the beast" (Rv 13:3-4). The terrible result: the beast gained absolute control over their lives. A second beast, a kind of unholy spirit, gives life to the son of Satan:

> *He was given power to give breath to the image of the first beast, so that it could speak and cause all who refused to worship the image to be killed. He also forced everyone, small and great, rich and poor, free and slave, to receive a mark on his right hand or on his forehead, so that no one could buy or sell unless he had the mark.*
>
> REVELATIONS 13:15-17

As we've seen throughout this book, worship is not just the songs you sing. It's the submission of your whole life and every part of it to a higher power, and that higher power *must be* the God of Scripture. Jesus makes plain: "No one can serve two masters. Either he will hate the one and love the other, or he will be devoted to the one and despise the other. You cannot serve both God and Money" (Mt 6:24).

The Greek term Jesus uses for "money" is *mamonas,* or "mammon." One of the standard New Testament Greek reference books tells us that this word comes from an Aramaic root that means "that in which one trusts."[1] Of course, whatever you devote yourself to, whatever you praise and worship, that's what you'll trust. The object of your "worship," that is, the things to which you attribute great worth, will become the focus of your "faith," and what you worship, whatever you give your life to, will rule your life. It could be alcohol or sex or your job or money, or just about anything other than God.

Gates of Praise

How important are praise and worship to God? In Psalm 87:2 we read that the Lord loves the gates of Zion more than all the dwellings of Jacob. *All* the dwellings *of Jacob?!* Imagine that! We might expect the psalmist to write that God loves the gates of Zion more than all the dwellings of Egypt or Assyria. But instead, he compares God's feelings about Zion, or Jerusalem, with his feelings about the other cities and villages of Jacob— that is, Israel.

What does this mean, that God favors Zion over the other dwellings of Israel? Isn't God omnipresent? Why would he prefer one place to another? Because, as the Bible teaches, God is particular about where he reveals his *special* presence, the *shekinah*. And the *shekinah* could be found in only one place: above the ark of the covenant in the Holy of Holies in the tabernacle and later in the temple. In conjunction with this, God's special *shekinah* presence in the Old Testament became inseparably identified with Jerusalem, or Zion, the capital city and spiritual stronghold of the nation of Israel.

Psalm 87 tells us specifically that God loves *the gates* of Zion more than all the dwellings of Jacob. What's up with that? What is it about those gates that is so appealing to God? The prophet Isaiah tells us: "Arise, shine [Jerusalem, Zion], for your light has come, and the glory of the Lord [the *shekinah*, his special presence] rises upon you.... You will call your walls Salvation and your gates Praise" (Is 60:1, 18).

Praise is the gateway into the presence of God. In another place the psalmist declares, "Shout for joy to the Lord, all the earth. Worship the Lord with gladness; come before him with joyful songs.... Enter his gates with thanksgiving and his courts with praise" (Ps 100:1-2, 4).

The Weapon of Praise

Gates are not only entry points, they're also a biblical symbol of authority and power. Many times in the Old Testament, for example, city leaders sat down at the city gates to make important decisions. Listen to this fascinating promise to Rebekah and her son, Jacob: "And they blessed Rebekah and said to her, 'Our sister, may you increase to thousands upon thousands; may your offspring possess the gates of their enemies'" (Gn 24:60). So, in the context of Bible history and culture, "gates" represent places of power and control.

In the New Testament, Jesus resolved to build his church on the rock of his life and ministry, and he promised that the "gates of Hades" would not prevail against her. I refer again to one of the most widely respected New Testament Greek references:

> *The most likely meaning is that the gates of Hades stand for*
> *the ungodly forces of the underworld which attack the rock*
> *but cannot prevail against it. Later the "gates of Hades"*
> *figure especially in references to Christ's descent into Hades,*
> *over whose gates he has supreme power.*[2]

Indeed, with eyes of fire the resurrected Christ decrees, "I am
the Living One; I was dead, and behold I am alive for ever and
ever! And I hold the keys of death and Hades" (Rv 1:18). It is
in this context that Psalm 127:5 takes on special meaning:
"Blessed is the man whose quiver is full [of children]. They will
not be put to shame when they contend with their enemies in
the gate." This suggests that gates are not only symbolic of
authority but they also represent the place where that authority
can be challenged. Worship is kingdom activity, and praise
allows us to possess the gates of our enemies.

Binding and Loosing

Perhaps nothing teaches the power of praise more clearly than
Psalm 149. The whole thrust of this passage is the primacy and
power of praise and worship, but it ends with one of the most
extraordinary statements in the Bible:

> *May the praise of God be in their mouths and a double-edged*
> *sword in their hands, to inflict vengeance on the nations and*
> *punishment on the peoples, to bind their kings with fetters,*
> *their nobles with shackles of iron, to carry out the sentence*
> *written against them. This is the glory of all his saints.*
>
> PSALM 149:6-9

Astounding! *Praise is a weapon.* Of course, the terms "kings" and "nobles" must be understood spiritually. These are not world rulers, literally, but the dark powers around them. By wielding the Word and worshiping, we have in our hands and in our mouths the power to overcome the dominion of darkness that holds the nations in its oppressive grip. By worshiping, we actually participate in God's purposes for the nations of the earth: "This is the glory of all his saints." This principle underlies the "Make Way" music of the wonderful songwriter and worship leader Graham Kendrick, whose best-known chorus is...

Shine, Jesus, shine
   Fill this land with the Father's glory.
Blaze, Spirit, blaze
   Set our hearts on fire.
Flow, River, flow
   Flood the nations with grace and mercy.[3]

The Hebrew term translated "glory" (the *glory* of the saints) in Psalm 150 is *hadar,* which means "ornament" or "splendor." According to R. Laird Harris in *Theological Wordbook of the Old Testament,* this word is associated with, among other things, the glory of nature and man as they reflect the glory and goodness of God. When we use praise as a weapon to bind Satan's power on the earth, we are fulfilling God's purpose for creating humans: to have dominion (see Gn 1:26). This same Hebrew word is used in Psalm 8:4-6: "What is man that you are mindful of him?... You ... crowned him with glory and honor [*hadar*]. You made him ruler over the works of your hands; you put everything under his feet."

It's the great honor of the saints to represent God on the

earth by exercising authority over the dominion of darkness. Right after his promise to us that the gates of hell would not prevail against the church, Jesus gave us an authority commission not unlike Psalm 149, to *bind:* "I will give you the keys of the kingdom of heaven; whatever you bind on earth will be bound in heaven, and whatever you loose on earth will be loosed in heaven" (Mt 16:19).

Psalm 47:1-3 shows the interface of praise and spiritual warfare, too: "Clap your hands, all you nations; shout to God with cries of joy.... He subdued nations under us, peoples under our feet." Praise and worship and the Word are alternating links in the chain that binds Satan and the forces of hell. *Praise is kingdom activity.*

Praise and the Coming of the Spirit

As we learned in an earlier chapter, the *shekinah* in the Old Testament was, in fact, the presence and power of the Third Person of the Trinity, the Holy Spirit, and where you have the presence of the Holy Spirit, you have God's power and kingdom. For forty days after his resurrection, Jesus spoke with his disciples about the kingdom of God (see Acts 1:3), at which time he promised, "You will receive power [kingdom authority] when the Holy Spirit comes on you" (Acts 1:8).

A few days later, just as Jesus had predicted, the Spirit of God fell on the disciples during the Jewish festival of Pentecost. People for blocks around heard a commotion, like a "violent wind" (Acts 2:2), and the disciples spoke in tongues. Often overlooked, though, is that spontaneous worship was also a sign of the coming of the power of the Spirit, for as they spoke in tongues, people could hear "them declaring the wonders of God in our own tongues!" (Acts 2:11).

So the dwelling place of God's special presence in the New Testament is his worshiping church. Pentecost is the special presence of God to empower Christians to do the work of the kingdom. Pentecost is also the rich experience of spiritual worship. It's no coincidence, then, that the global revival of the Christian faith and the worldwide outpouring of the Holy Spirit over the last twenty-five years have been so centered, not in speaking in tongues, but in worship. When people worship, the Spirit comes in power, and when the Spirit comes in power, *worship!* Satan is cast down!

A Case Study of Praise and Warfare

If you are in a spiritual battle, read the incredible story of warfare and victory in 2 Chronicles 20. Notice especially the importance of praise and worship in verses 18-22:

> Jehoshaphat bowed with his face to the ground, and all the people of Judah and Jerusalem fell down in worship before the Lord. Then some Levites from the Kohathites and Korahites stood up and praised the Lord, the God of Israel, with very loud voice. Early in the morning they left for the Desert of Tekoa.
>
> As they set out, Jehoshaphat stood and said, "Listen to me, Judah and people of Jerusalem! Have faith in the Lord your God and you will be upheld; have faith in his prophets and you will be successful."
>
> After consulting the people, Jehoshaphat appointed

men to sing to the Lord and to praise him for the splendor of his holiness as they went out at the head of the army, saying: "Give thanks to the Lord, for his love endures forever." As they began to sing and praise, the Lord set ambushes against the men of Ammon and Moab and Mount Seir who were invading Judah, and they were defeated.

After reading and meditating on this Jehoshaphat narrative, pray and affirm one or more of the following triumphant kingdom Psalms: 2, 46, 47, 100, 110. Speak these psalms aloud as a confession to build your faith. Speak them aloud to the audiences of heaven, earth, and hell. Do it daily, or even several times a day, if you need to.

Praise and the Coming Kingdom

Old Testament prophecy even suggests that the establishment of the messianic kingdom will be uniquely characterized by praise and worship. When the future kingdom is fully established, the ultimate issue of the universe—worship—will be resolved forever. Never again will the hearts of men and angels bow every which way, except before God.

Psalm 102 points forward to a new nation of God's people headquartered in the heavenly Jerusalem: "You will arise and have compassion on Zion, for it is time to show favor to her; the appointed time has come" (v. 13). At this time, "the nations will fear the name of the Lord, all the kings of the earth will revere your glory.... So the name of the Lord will be declared in Zion and his praise in Jerusalem when the peoples and the kingdoms assemble to worship the Lord" (vv. 15, 21-22).

This prophecy has a twofold significance. First, it promises that the gospel of the kingdom will be preached to all nations. No longer will Jehovah's influence be limited to little Israel, but the fame of his name will cover the earth as the waters cover the sea. This happens when we obey the Great Commission to disciple the nations.

Second, the prophecy of Psalm 102 points toward the ultimate and total triumph of Christ over the nations, when the reign and rule of God will be established in a new heaven and a new earth. All the groaning from the weight of sin will be silenced as the whole creation is released into the liberty of Christ. All the earth will bow down in unrestrained worship, and the kingdom of God will be established forever.

No longer will there be two masters. Satan will be thrown into the lake of fire forever. Paul puts it this way: "Therefore God exalted him [Jesus] to the highest place and gave him the name that is above every name, that at the name of Jesus every knee should bow, in heaven and on earth and under the earth" (Phil 2:9-10).

Until the Grand Ending, however, the kingdom is among us and at hand. As Ron Ford has written, "We are living in *the presence of the future*.... The Kingdom of God *is* where the rule and reign of God is exercised and made visible."[4] And the reign of God is made visible where people worship in word and deed.

Worship is the ultimate issue of the universe. Worship is perhaps the most powerful and liberating weapon in the armory of God. Worship affirms the lordship of Jesus Christ over all creation and casts down the dominion of darkness.[5]

Sing praises to God, sing praises;
* sing praises to our King, sing praises.*
For God is the King of all the earth;
* sing to him a psalm of praise.*
God reigns over the nations;
* God is seated on his holy throne.*

PSALM 47:6-8

TEN

PRACTICING PRAISE

You are not discouraged, unless the problem you face is bigger than the God you worship. How big is your God?

Anonymous

Not long ago we were wildly celebrating the beginning of a new century. The economy was bullying its way forward in record leaps and bounds, and the future seemed as bright as the massive New Year's Eve fireworks displays from Sydney to San Francisco.

Today everything has changed. Suddenly, we find ourselves rethinking our futures and longing for the safety and security of a world that's left us forever. Everything about tomorrow seems less certain, and the images of September 11, 2001, suggest that our world will never be the same.

The world, however, has *always* been like this, and the World Trade Center tragedy is not some radically new evil on the dark side of human history. We've just forgotten that ten million people died in World War I and fifty million in World War II. The recent attack on America, though, is a wake-up call, a terrifying metaphor for how fragile our world really is, even its most enduring symbols, like the tallest buildings in New York, the Pentagon, or the Capitol. Or even the United States of America.

Yes, in some ways things seem normal again. Just take a drive down to your local mall or Wal-Mart. Watch the thousands of people, mostly young people, going to movies and restaurants. Yet if you talk to them about their money, their future, you'll find that they're feeling afraid.

Over thirty years ago, a Christian leader by the name of Merlin Carothers wrote a best-selling book entitled *Prison to Praise*. It's still available, and the message of the book is timeless. Praise isn't just something you do with a group of people in church. It's a key that unlocks the prison of your personal circumstances and releases you into the freedom of God's blessings for your future.

> *Therefore let everyone who is godly pray to you while you may be found; surely when the mighty waters rise, they will not reach him. You are my hiding place; you will protect me from trouble and surround me with songs of deliverance.*
>
> PSALM 32:6-7

Praise is a partner of prayer, and *praise is practical!* Whatever comes against your life, you can praise and worship in the ugly face of your trouble, knowing that the power of God's special glory and presence will carry you through. This, essentially, is the message of Psalm 66, an ancient step-by-step instruction manual on how to put praise into practice, so this last chapter in my book is interactive. Don't just read it. Do it! This marvelous Psalm has five parts, which I've summarized with "praise principles."

PRAISE PRINCIPLE #1: If you are troubled or afraid, worship God for who he is.

Shout with joy to God, all the earth! (v. 1).

Shout to God. OK, do you think you're willing to try this? Obeying the Bible is never a bad thing to do, but sometimes the Bible tells us to do things that might make us feel uncomfortable. You might have to find a place where you can do this. Like out in the country. Or in your apartment with all the windows closed. You might feel a little awkward, and you don't have to shout yourself hoarse, but lifting your voice in passion to God can be healing for your soul, as it was for Jabez, who "cried out to the God of Israel, 'Oh, that you would bless me!'" (1 Chr 4:10).

Did you know that in the world-famous corporate prayer meetings in churches across Korea, people pray in unison so loudly that they have to have a huge prayer bell? No, not to call people to pray, but to signal the time when they should stop!

Sing the glory of his name; make his praise glorious! (v. 2).

Sing about his glorious name. Write down all the names of God you can think of in the Bible. Or use the Psalms. Or get yourself a Bible program for your computer and do a search for the word "name" in the Psalms. You might be able to find information like this on the Internet. A great Bible study site on the Web is http://unbound.biola.edu. Once you've assembled your list, use those names in your prayers and praise, meditating on what each one might mean for you in your unique situation.

Hanging above my desk in my church office is a gift from my

dear wife done with her own tender hands, a framed cross-stitch of seven of the "I am's" of Jesus, like, "I am the resurrection and the life." Sometimes I just look at that and read it aloud. In some ways, there's no better way to pray and worship than to call out one name of Jesus after another!

> *Say to God, "How awesome are your deeds! So great is your power that your enemies cringe before you. All the earth bows down to you; they sing praise to you, they sing praise to your name." Selah (v. 3-4).*

Go ahead, obey the command. Say it ... Remind yourself that God is in control by telling him that his power is great, his enemies cringe, and all the earth bows down. What in your life is not part of "all the earth"? What part of your life is outside the boundaries of God's power? Every knee will bow, Paul tells us in Philippians 2:10-11, and every tongue will confess that Jesus Christ is Lord.

When you praise God in the face of your trouble, you are putting your problem under the lordship of Christ. You are making Jesus Lord of your life and renouncing the power and lordship of the problem. You know, of course, that whatever determines how you feel and think and live is your god. So you can have a career god, a hobby god, a problem god. Or God.

***Selah,* that is, think about it deeply.** Now spend a few moments, perhaps with your eyes closed, thinking about each of the first four verses of Psalm 66.

PRAISE PRINCIPLE #2: If you are troubled or afraid, praise God for what he has done—in holy history and for you personally.

Come and see what God has done, how awesome his works in man's behalf! He turned the sea into dry land, they passed through the waters on foot—come, let us rejoice in him (v. 5-6).

Read again some of the great miracle narratives of the Old or New Testament. What comfort to know that the person writing Psalm 66 may have been right where you are, needing encouragement, desperate for deeper faith. It's not like the psalmist was watching the Red Sea miracle firsthand. He, too, was remembering what God had done for his people hundreds of years before. Just like you, he was centuries removed from the actual events, but what his family had told him about the miracles of Jahweh in the past helped make God real to him in the present.

The first Passover and the crossing of the Red Sea, pivotal events of the Old Testament, are symbols of salvation and baptism (see 1 Cor 10:2). In other words, if God can get you out of the slavery of Egypt, away from the bondage of your past, then he can get you through any wilderness that stands between you and the Promised Land! Paul picked up on this when he wrote, "For if, when we were God's enemies, we were reconciled to him through the death of his Son, how much more, having been reconciled, shall we be saved through his life!" (Rom 5:10).

Put a smile on your face, and "rejoice in him"! Praise remembers and sings about the acts of God, but worship centers on God himself: *"Rejoice in him."*

> *He rules forever by his power, his eyes watch the nations—let not the rebellious rise up against him.* Selah *(v. 7).*

Confess to yourself, silently or aloud, "God rules forever." God knows what's going down, and God will hold evil people responsible. Go back and read verse 7 again. Read it aloud.

Selah, think about it deeply. Spend a few more moments meditating about each of these last few verses of Psalm 66.

PRAISE PRINCIPLE #3: Praise is the way we welcome the refining processes of life.

> *Praise our God, O peoples, let the sound of his praise be heard; he has preserved our lives and kept our feet from slipping. For you, O God, tested us; you refined us like silver. You brought us into prison and laid burdens on our backs. You let men ride over our heads; we went through fire and water, but you brought us to a place of abundance (v. 8-12).*

Specifically thank God for whatever you can receive from him as a result of your difficulty and pain. Why? Because we will never grow into everything God has for us if we are not "forced" to trust him totally. Unfortunately, that only happens when we're helpless. God's best blessings are always at the very boundary of our limitations. Ever feel like you're on the edge?

Well, rejoice, because that's where you are about to meet God! God is always just over the edge!

God helps the helpless. He doesn't meet us halfway. He meets us when we reach the end of ourselves, which is why the apostle Paul could write, "But he said to me, 'My grace is sufficient for you, for my power is made perfect in weakness.' Therefore I will boast all the more gladly about my weaknesses, so that Christ's power may rest on me" (2 Cor 12:9).

> Less of me, more of God.
> More of me, less of God.
> None of me, all of God.

You may never be able to bring yourself to thank God for the trouble or pain in your life, but you can *always* thank him for what he's going to do in you through it. Years ago, Christian recording artist Andre Crouch sang, "Through it all, I've learned to trust in Jesus. I've learned to trust in God."

Rejoice that God has preserved your life and kept your feet from slipping. God may not keep us *from* trouble, but he'll keep us *through* it: "No temptation has seized you except what is common to man. And God is faithful; he will not let you be tempted beyond what you can bear. But when you are tempted, he will also provide a way out so that you can stand up under it" (1 Cor 10:13). What kind of "way out" is that?! We would rather pray for God to take away the problem! Or take us out of it!

Yet God is not in the business of making bad things go away. He is, however, in the business of giving us all the grace we need to stand up to the worst things in life, whether or not they go away. Worship is a life jacket in the raging rapids of life. When the waters of the river of life get rough, God will keep you afloat in his life-saving presence. His promise to you is: "My God is sufficient for you, for my power is made perfect in weakness."

Acknowledge that, though God does not cause suffering, you can find him right in the middle of whatever happens. I personally am not convinced that God *causes* trouble, although Psalm 66 certainly implies that. Hebrews explains it this way: "Endure hardship as discipline; God is treating you as sons. For what son is not disciplined by his father?" (Heb 12:7). The simple message in this verse is this: whatever form hardship may take or whatever the cause, every adversity in life is an opportunity for us to allow God to discipline us, to discover what he wants us to learn. If nothing else, he always wants us to learn to trust him more.

So, whatever happens, no matter why it happens, God is always right there immediately present to encourage and help us. He "is our refuge and strength, an ever-present help in trouble" (Ps 46:1). The challenge, then, in every setback in life is to worship your way through the pain right into the loving arms of God.

When you are in pain, turn to God to see how he is going to work in your life through it. To me, this is one of the top two or three things we can learn in life and teach one another, but here's what we do, what our family and friends do when there's pain: we take it very personally and blame others. Sometimes we even blame God. I heard my friend Wellington Boone once say, "Ever notice how easy it is to see God working in somebody else's life? How easy it is to give them advice? And how hard it is for *them* to see it? And then how hard it is for *me* to see anything clearly when *I'm* going through it?"

We will never discover that all things are possible with God until we discover that most things are impossible for us. This is the act of accepting the refining process, praising God for it, and worshiping him through it. Tough times are the only times when I discover that I can do all things *only* through Christ, who strengthens me.

PRAISE PRINCIPLE #4: Worshiping God when everything is great is natural. Worshiping God when everything isn't great is unnatural. It's a "sacrifice of praise."

> *I will come to your temple with burnt offerings and fulfill my vows to you—vows my lips promised and my mouth spoke when I was in trouble. I will sacrifice fat animals to you and an offering of rams; I will offer bulls and goats.* Selah *(v. 13-15).*

Praise God even when you don't want to, even when it hurts. Years ago in our church, we sang a chorus,

> We bring the sacrifice of praise
> into the house of the Lord.
> And we offer up to you
> the sacrifices of thanksgiving.

A sacrifice of praise? That's a contradiction of terms! Shouldn't praise be the joyful, spontaneous response of the human soul to God? Well, yes, but sometimes it isn't. Sometimes praising God is the last thing I really want to do. Maybe that's what the old bumper sticker means: PRAISE THE LORD *ANYWAY*.

It's biblical to praise God when you have good reason to praise him. It's also biblical to praise God when you don't. Personally, I've found that it takes more faith for the latter! That's why Job's wife told him, "Curse God and die!" (Jb 2:9). In other words, "Job, you have no reason whatsoever to worship. In fact, to thank God right now seems like madness." Yet Job was determined to praise God. He may have sounded like Psalm 116:17, "I will *sacrifice* a thank offering to you and call on the name of the Lord."

Have you ever screamed, "THIS SITUATION IS KILLING ME!" Well, it probably is. You are dying to self, and self doesn't like dying. More of God always means less of you, as John the Baptist understood, "He [Jesus] must become greater; I must become less" (Jn 3:30). In the most difficult times in my life, just like a lamb bleeding to death on the altar of sacrifice, I want to shriek, "I DON'T NEED THIS IN MY LIFE!" Yet I've discovered that the fastest way through the pain is, first, to reach outside of myself for more of God's sustaining grace, and, second, to search deeply inside my own heart to discover what God is saying to me, to identify things in me that need adjustment or change.

Paul wrote about it this way: "Therefore, I urge you, brothers, in view of God's mercy, to offer your bodies as living sacrifices, holy and pleasing to God—this is your spiritual act of worship" (Rom 12:1).

Selah, think about it deeply. Spend a few more moments meditating about each of these verses of Psalm 66. If you are in a difficult place in your life right now, think about what God may want you to learn from the hardship. If you can't think of something, ask someone very close to you what he or she thinks. And listen to that person!

Make a list of what you "hear" from God in your heart as you wait quietly in his presence. After making the list, pray for God to fulfill each and every one of his specific purposes for your life. Don't pray *against* your adversary. Press into God for what he wants to do in you.

PRAISE PRINCIPLE #5: Worship is being positive, living right, and staying faithful.

Come and listen, all you who fear God; let me tell you what he has done for me (v. 16).

Don't just tell others about your problems. Tell them about how God is working in your life! How novel! How seldom we do this! I don't have to tell you that complaining about your problems only makes matters worse, and usually drags all the people who are close to you into the darkness of your personal hell. Imagine, if in every conversation about our troubles, we made "sacrifices of praise and thanksgiving" by telling others how God was working all things together for our good! What a breath of fresh air that would be! Our world and the whole world would be a much better place!

Often, though, instead of searching our souls and pressing deeper into God for grace and strength, we persist in making things worse for ourselves and others by talking about how hurt we are, how unfair it is, how victimized we feel. Negativity is emotional quicksand. The more negative you become, the deeper you go and the faster you get there. Self-pity is emotionally suffocating.

You know, you can't pull yourself out of quicksand, and the more you struggle, the worse it gets. Stop fighting it! Just calm your troubled soul and let God pull you out, and that will happen when you stop complaining and start praising, like the psalmist ...

> *I cried out to him with my mouth; his praise was on my tongue. If I had cherished sin in my heart, the Lord would not have listened (v. 17-18).*

Worship God with your whole life. Never forget what we've been considering all though this book: Worship is not just what you do in church, it's who you are on Monday and every other day of the week. Even if you've never done it, lifting your hands or shouting to God is the easy part. Living for God every day, obeying his Word, worshiping him while you work, now there's a challenge or two!

Never forget: you're not alone. God isn't some neutral force, waiting to see what you are going to do. Jesus in you is up to the challenge. He's there to help you in your weakness (see Rom 8:26), and if God is for us, who can be against us? This is certainly why Psalm 66 ends this way ...

> *But God has surely listened and heard my voice in prayer. Praise be to God, who has not rejected my prayer or withheld his love from me! (v. 19-20)*

That's a pretty good ending for this book, too.

NOTES

One
One Thing More Than Anything

1. *New International Dictionary of the New Testament.*

Two
Behold Your God!

1. This is the term "mammon" in the old King James Bible, and yes, "Money" is capitalized in the NIV, just like "God."
2. For those of you readers who are not American, whether or not you like it, for good or for evil, American values are "colonizing" global culture, so you need to think about how American ideas may be influencing how you think about God.
3. J.B. Phillips, *Your God Is Too Small*; Donald McCullough, *The Trivialization of God: The Dangerous Illusion of a Manageable Deity.*
4. R. Laird Harris, *Theological Wordbook of the Old Testament.*
5. I have come to define the judgment of God in terms of the consequences of our own self-destructive behaviors. God's judgment is built right into the universe he's created. From sex to gravity, the more you defy the laws of God, the greater the potential consequences. For example, conservative radio talk show host Dr. Laura Schlessinger has stated that, in her view, the effects of divorce last seventy-five years.
6. Harris.

Three
Holy Awe

1. *The Knowledge of the Holy.*
2. Over the course of church history, people have come up with some very wrong, nonbiblical ideas about the Trinity. Two of these are *subordinationism,* which says that Christ is divine but less than God, and *adoptionism,* which holds that Christ was only a human being, temporarily endowed with God's Spirit while he was alive on earth. This second view is very close to what the Mormons believe. Again, both of these heresies, in effect, deny that God himself *personally* entered human history. *Modalism,* on the other hand, holds the Persons of Christ and the Holy Spirit to be only historical roles or *modes,* which is a little like saying that there is only one God who just wears different hats.
3. More biblical references to the Trinity: (1) the baptism "formula" of Matthew 28:19; (2) the blessing of the apostle Paul in 2 Corinthians 13:14; (3) at least seven references to Jesus as God in the New Testament, including John 1:18, John 20:28, and Titus 2:13; and (4) many references to the Holy Spirit as God in the New Testament, including Acts 5:3.
4. "Incarnation" means, literally, "enfleshment," and is the theological word for God becoming a man in the human person of Jesus of Nazareth, conceived by the Holy Spirit, born of the Virgin Mary.

Four
You Had to Be There

1. Many conservative Christians use the term "propositional truth" to refer to the unchanging, objective truths of the Bible. In other words, the truth of the Bible can be understood as propositions, statements of unarguable absolutes, against which all life experiences must be measured.

2. God's omnipresence, of course, is not to be confused with pantheism, the pagan and increasingly popular notion of a divine force in and around every stone and bush, that God is the sum total of the universe and all of us in it. Yes, God is everywhere in his creation, but God is separate from the created order. He is transcendent, something we discussed in the previous chapter.

Five
Transformation

1. Gerhard Kittel and Gerhard Friedrich, *Theological Dictionary of the New Testament,* translated and abridged in one volume by Geoffrey W. Bromily (Grand Rapids, Mich.: William B. Eerdmans, 1985), 636–39.

2. The Greek term translated "transformed" in Romans 12:2 is *metamorpho-o,* which means, literally, to change the form, which is why the term has made it into the language of biology, referring specifically to the form change that takes place when a caterpillar becomes a butterfly. It's a *metamorphosis.* How appropriate for describing the change in us

when we are born again and given a new "form" as our old nature dies with Christ and we are resurrected with a brand new nature.

3. Contemplate how any of several biblical terms can be used interchangeably, how "the presence of God," "the glory of God," and the *shekinah* are simply other terms for the Holy Spirit. Try each of the four phrases at the beginning of any of the statements below:

The presence of God ...
The glory of God ...
The *shekinah* ...
The Holy Spirit ...

      ... was in the burning bush, calling Moses to ministry.

      ... was reflected on the face of Moses.

      ... was in the wilderness of Sinai, a cloud by day and a fire by night.

      ... was hovering above the ark in the tabernacle of Moses.

      ... was returning to the tabernacle of David in Zion.

      ... was in the temple of Solomon.

      ... was pouring out of the temple in Ezekiel's vision of the river of life (see Ez 47:1-9).

      ... was falling on Jesus at his Baptism.

      ... was falling on the believers in the Upper Room on the day of Pentecost.

      ... is what we encounter when we worship in Spirit and in truth.

      ... is in my clay jar and pouring out of my soul like a river of life (see Jn 7:38-39).

4. Sally Morganthaler, *Worship Evangelism: Inviting Unbelievers into the Presence of God* (Grand Rapids, Mich.: Zondervan, 1999), 52-53.

5. John Chisum, "Worship's Bottom Line," *Ministries Today* July/August 1995, 57.

Six
Perfect Jesus, Take My Hand

1. Notice that one phrase appears in all of these verses: "Praise the Lord." That's really all you need to memorize for today. Did you think I was serious about having you memorize all these verses? Do I hear a sigh of relief?

2. I refer here to the *New International Version* (NIV).

3. Yes, this is a play on words, a juggling of a rather negative counseling term and the idea expressed in the King James Old Testament where we are encouraged to have our hearts "fixed on" (stuck on, attached to) God.

Seven
Wholehearted, Full-Bodied Praise

1. By introducing the word "sensual" I'm not suggesting that worship is sensual in terms of the way the word is now commonly used to mean sexual experience, but in terms of feelings, passion, and literally the experience of the five senses.

2. Thanks to Jack Hayford for this little phrase, "wholehearted and full-bodied."

3. I compiled this list with the help of my Worship and Arts staff. Literally, we've heard every one of these things. Some often.
4. I had a friend tell me once that his off-the-wall interpretation of those thirty silent minutes was that God, like a harried parent, was saying something like, "I can't take all this arguing anymore! I want peace! For just thirty minutes!"
5. "Liturgy" is derived from the New Testament Greek word translated "worship." "Vespers" is church in the evening.

Eight
Monday Worship

1. A wonderful book on work as a calling is *The Call,* by Os Guinness.
2. You can read about Moses and his goat stick (that's my term!) in Exodus 3.
3. Enron is the multi-billion dollar Texas corporation whose financial collapse was fueled by questionable accounting practices.

Nine
Warfare Worship

1. Aramaic, a kind of Hebrew dialect, was the common language spoken by Jesus and his disciples. See Kittel and Friedrich, 55.
2. Kittel and Friedrich, 974–75, italics added.

3. Graham Kendrick, Copyright 1987, Make Way Music, P.O. Box 263, Croydon, Surrey, CR9 5AP, U.K. International copyright secured. All rights reserved. Used by permission.

4. Ron Ford, "The Powerful Advance of God's Kingdom in the Earth," *First Fruits,* January–February 1986, 16.

5. Much of this chapter has been taken from the author's book *Overcoming the Dominion of Darkness* (Grand Rapids, Mich.: Baker/Chosen, 1989), which is being republished by Vine books. The out-of-print edition can still be ordered through our church Internet bookstore: www.wordofgrace.org.

The Beginner's Guide Series

The Beginner's Guide to Spiritual Warfare
by Neil T. Anderson

The Beginner's Guide to the Gift of Prophecy
by Jack Deere

The Beginner's Guide to Intercession
by Dutch Sheets

The Beginner's Guide to Receiving the Holy Spirit
by Quin Sherrer and Ruthanne Garlock

The Beginner's Guide to Spiritual Gifts
by Sam Storms

The Beginner's Guide to Fasting
by Elmer Towns

**Ask for them at your nearest Christian bookstore,
or go to www.servantpub.com.**